JOHN McGARRY was born in Belfast, Northern Ireland. He grew up in Ballymena, County Antrim. He was educated at St MacNissi's College, Garron Tower, County Antrim, Trinity College Dublin and at the University of Western Ontario, Canada. He was a Professor and Head of the Department of Politics at King's College, University of Western Ontario (1989–98), and is now Professor of Political Science at the University of Waterloo, Canada. He is a specialist in national and ethnic conflict regulation, and a regular contributor to public media.

BRENDAN O'LEARY was born in Cork, Ireland. He grew up in Nigeria, Northern Ireland and the Sudan. He was educated at St MacNissi's College, Garron Tower, County Antrim, Oxford University and the LSE, where he is now Professor of Political Science and Head of the Department of Government. He has been a political adviser to Dr Marjorie Mowlam and Kevin McNamara, a constitutional consultant to the European Union and the United Nations, and is a regular broadcaster on British, Irish and American networks.

OTHER BOOKS BY THE AUTHORS

The Asiatic Mode of Production (O'Leary, 1989)
Explaining Northern Ireland: Broken Images (McGarry and O'Leary, 1995)
The Future of Northern Ireland (McGarry and O'Leary, eds., 1990)
Northern Ireland: Sharing Authority (O'Leary, Tom Lyne, Jim Marshall
  and Bob Rowthorn, 1993)
The Politics of Antagonism: Understanding Northern Ireland (O'Leary and
  McGarry, 1993 and 1996)
The Politics of Ethnic Conflict Regulation (McGarry and O'Leary, eds.,
  1993)
Prime Minister, Cabinet and Core Executive (special issue of *Public
  Administration*, O'Leary, Patrick Dunleavy and R.A.W. Rhodes,
  eds., 1990)
State of Truce: Northern Ireland After Twenty-five Years of War (special issue
  of *Ethnic and Racial Studies*, O'Leary and McGarry, eds., 1995)
Theories of the State: The Politics of Liberal Democracy (O'Leary and Patrick
  Dunleavy, 1987)

POLICING
NORTHERN IRELAND
Proposals for a new start

JOHN McGARRY & BRENDAN O'LEARY

THE
BLACKSTAFF
PRESS
———
BELFAST

First published in 1999 by
The Blackstaff Press Limited
Blackstaff House, Wildflower Way, Apollo Road, Belfast BT12 6TA, Northern Ireland

Typeset by Techniset Typesetters, Newton-le-Willows, Merseyside

Printed in Ireland by ColourBooks Limited

A CIP catalogue record for this book
is available from the British Library

ISBN 0-85640-648-1

dedicated to all the makers,
great and small,
of the British–Irish Agreement of
10 April 1998

Contents

Acknowledgements

We would especially like to thank the following for reading the entire manuscript, and making valuable suggestions: Pia Chaudhuri of the Department of Government at the London School of Economics and Political Science, Mike Brogden of the Institute of Criminology and Criminal Justice at Queen's University in Belfast, Brice Dickson of the University of Ulster's law faculty, and Margaret Moore of the Department of Political Science at the University of Waterloo, Canada.

Many people have helped John McGarry, especially during a field trip in 1998, and Brendan O'Leary, both recently and over many years, not all of whom can be named here – though not because of any views police officers might have about them. Those who must be named include Maggie Beirne and Martin O'Brien of the Committee for the Administration of Justice, Keith Bryett and Kieran McEvoy of the Institute of Criminology and Criminal Justice at Queen's University, and Pat Conway of the Northern Ireland Association for the Care and Re-settlement of Offenders. John Bradley of the Economic and Social Research Institute, Dublin, Dr Diarmuid Ó Mathúna of the Dublin Institute for Advanced Studies, and Kathleen Cavanagh of Queen's University, Belfast, were also very helpful.

People who assisted McGarry in Canada include Sergeant Graham Bunting of the Stratford Police, Karlene Hussey of the Ontario Civilian Commissioners of Police Services, M. Noel Kelly, and Professors Michael Keating and Allan McDougall of the Department of Political Science at the University of Western Ontario. McGarry would like to thank the Social Science and Humanities Research Council of Canada for financial assistance.

People who aided O'Leary include Katharine Adeney, Brian Feeney, Pia Chaudhuri and Amanda Francis – the last two were particularly helpful in proofing a text that was produced at high speed first in London, Canada, and then in London, England. Geoffrey Evans of Nuffield College, Oxford, data-dredged and found errors with his eagle eyes. The Essex University data archive team was very professional at short notice. Jane Pugh of LSE's drawing office delivered the figures with her customary professionalism. LSE's staff research fund assisted some last-minute activity. We would like to thank Blackstaff Press for taking this proposal at short notice, and for finishing it with meticulous professionalism.

Both McGarry and O'Leary would especially like to thank the United States Institute of Peace for financial help with research.

JOHN McGARRY AND BRENDAN O'LEARY
LONDON, ONTARIO, AND LONDON, ENGLAND
30 OCTOBER 1998

Glossary

Catholic is a shorthand expression for a believer in the doctrines of the Holy Roman Catholic and Apostolic Church; it is not a synonym for an Irish nationalist, although most Catholics are nationalists. In this book we generally use 'Catholics' to mean 'cultural Catholics', that is, to refer to practising Catholics as well as persons born into the Roman Catholic religion who no longer believe or practise its tenets.

Consociation is the name of a political system used in some deeply divided territories to share and divide governmental power and authority. In a consociation there is cross-community executive power-sharing, and proportional representation of groups in the executive, in the legislature and in all public employment. Each community is autonomous in the management of its culture and has effective rights of veto. The British–Irish Agreement of 1998 establishes a consociational system for the internal government of Northern Ireland.

Dáil Éireann is the lower house of the parliament of the Republic of Ireland.

Derry/Londonderry is the second city of Northern Ireland. Irish nationalists call it Derry, most unionists who live outside the city call it Londonderry, and in official designations both names have been used.

Éire is the official constitutional name for Ireland in the Irish language. It was given this name in Bunreacht na hÉireann (Ireland's 1937 Constitution).

Federal relationships may exist when more than one tier of government or administration exists in the same territory and where no tier has the unilateral right to alter the powers or competencies of the others – one can have federal government but one can also have federal policing.

Great Britain is that part of the United Kingdom that excludes Northern Ireland: it is more accurate than the partisan term 'the British mainland'. Northern Ireland is part of the United Kingdom, but it is not part of Great Britain, and to describe it as exclusively British, either geographically or administratively, is to beg political questions. There are British people in Northern Ireland but that does not make it exclusively British, although it helps explain why it is part of the United Kingdom.

Integration   is the attempt to organise a territory and its peoples under one unified set of political norms. Two main types of integration are advocated for Northern Ireland: into Britain and into Ireland.

(1)   Integration into Britain: *Administrative integration* would ensure that Northern Ireland is administered like Great Britain (or like England, or like Scotland, or like Wales), for example by having the same policing arrangements; *electoral integration* would mean that all Great Britain's political parties would compete for support in Northern Ireland; while *educational integration* would ensure that Protestants and Catholics attended the same schooling institutions.

(2)   Integration into Ireland: *Administrative integration* would mean that Northern Ireland was incorporated into the unitary Republic of Ireland; *electoral integration* would mean that the Republic's political parties competed for support in Northern Ireland; and *educational integration* would ensure that Protestants and Catholics attended the same schooling institutions.

Integrationists   support at least one type of integration (administrative, electoral or educational) and (with the exception of educational integrationists) are hostile to consociation (q.v.) or federal (q.v.) relationships.

Ireland   We use 'Ireland' to refer to the geographical entity, or the unit of administration before 1920, and we recognise that Ireland is the official constitutional name of the Republic of Ireland in the English language (Constitution of Ireland, Article 4). Since the British–Irish Agreement of 1998, to which both unionists (q.v.) and nationalists (q.v.) are parties, the term 'the South' is now a recognised synonym for the Republic of Ireland.

Irish Free State   is the name of the independent Irish state established in 1922, which acquired full sovereignty in 1937, and was declared a Republic in 1949. We use the expression to refer to independent Ireland between 1922 and 1937.

Nationalist   in this book refers to an Irish nationalist, usually a cultural Catholic. Although most Ulster unionists (q.v.) are British nationalists, for clarity we do not call them nationalists.

North   'the North', has usually been one of nationalists' preferred designations for Northern Ireland. Since the British–Irish Agreement of 1998, to which both unionists and nationalists are parties, the term 'the North' is now an officially recognised synonym for Northern Ireland.

Northern Ireland   is the name of the formal political unit created by the

Government of Ireland Act, not the 'Six Counties' or 'Ulster' as nationalists and unionists respectively prefer to describe it. Since the British–Irish Agreement of 1998, the term 'the North' is now an officially recognised synonym for Northern Ireland.

Others   is the new official designation for those persons and parties that choose to register as neither nationalist nor unionist in the new Northern Ireland Assembly.

Paramilitaries   meaning members of illegal or semi-legal armies, is a more precise and less emotive term than 'terrorists'. Both state officials and insurgents can practise terrorism – although 'terrorist' has almost exclusively been used to refer to insurgent paramilitaries.

Protestant   in this book is a shorthand expression for somebody who is a believer in the doctrines of one of the many Protestant (including Presbyterian) churches in Northern Ireland, or for cultural Protestants, that is, those who have Protestant religious backgrounds. 'Protestant' is not a synonym for 'unionist', although most Protestants are unionists.

The *Republic of Ireland*   is the formal political unit established in 1949. We use 'the Republic' as shorthand, and avoid the derogatory use of the terms 'the Free State' or 'the Twenty-six Counties'.

South   usually 'the South', is a shorthand expression for the Republic of Ireland. Since the British–Irish Agreement of 1998, to which both unionists (q.v.) and nationalists (q.v.) are parties, the term 'the South' is now an officially recognised synonym for the Republic of Ireland.

Ulster   properly speaking is 'historical Ulster', that is, the province that encompassed nine counties of pre-1920 Ireland; we do not use it as a synonym for Northern Ireland, although Northern Ireland's unionists normally do.

Unionist   with a capital 'U' refers to a member of one of the parties that bear this name, whereas with a lower-case 'u' it refers to anybody who believes in preserving the United Kingdom of Great Britain and Northern Ireland.

Unitary   arrangements exist when sub-central governments or administrative units enjoy no autonomous constitutional authority – their authority is revocable at the discretion of the central authorities.

Abbreviations

AIA	Anglo-Irish Agreement
AOH	Ancient Order of Hibernians
APNI	Alliance Party of Northern Ireland – it supports power-sharing devolved government within the Union as well as an Irish dimension
BIA	British–Irish Agreement of 10 April 1998, also known as 'the Agreement', or 'the Good Friday Agreement'
BIIC	British–Irish Intergovernmental Council
CAJ	Committee for the Administration of Justice
CPLC(s)	Community–Police Liaison Committee(s)
CSTE	Córas Síochána Thuaisceart Éireann, Gaelic name proposed in this book as an idiomatic translation of 'Northern Ireland Police Service'
CIRA	Continuity IRA, breakaway paramilitary faction from (Provisional) IRA, not on cease-fire as this book went to press
DUP	Democratic Unionist Party, hardline loyalist political party, formed and still led by the Reverend Ian Paisley MEP MP; opposed to the 1998 British–Irish Agreement
EPA	Emergency Provisions Act
FEC	Fair Employment Commission
FET	Fair Employment Tribunal
GAA	Gaelic Athletic Association
INLA	Irish National Liberation Army, Marxist and republican paramilitary organisation
IRA	Irish Republican Army (see PIRA), a name first given to Irish Volunteers in the Irish war of independence (1919–21), then used by anti-Treaty forces in the Irish civil war, now used by the illegal paramilitary organisation, on cease-fire as this book went to press.
IRB	Irish Republican Brotherhood, one of the predecessors of the IRA
LVF	Loyalist Volunteer Force, breakaway paramilitary faction from the UVF, on cease-fire as this book went to press
NIPS	Northern Ireland Police Service, umbrella name for the RUC,

	traffic wardens and civilian employees of the Police Authority for Northern Ireland, proposed in this book as the new name for an upper-tier policing service
NIO	Northern Ireland Office
NIWC	Northern Ireland Women's Coalition, a new political party that designates itself as neither nationalist nor unionist, but as both and 'other', led by Monica McWilliams
OO	Orange Order
PANI	Police Authority for Northern Ireland
PIRA	Provisional IRA, an illegal republican paramilitary organisation, formed in 1969–70, on cease-fire as this book went to press. Also known as IRA.
PR	Proportional representation
PTA	Prevention of Terrorism Act
PUP	Progressive Unionist Party, loyalist political party with historical links to the UVF, led by David Ervine
RCMP	Royal Canadian Mounted Police
RIRA	Real IRA, breakaway paramilitary faction from the IRA, on cease-fire as this book went to press
RSF	Republican Sinn Féin, breakaway fraction from SF, formed in 1986
RUC	Royal Ulster Constabulary
SACHR	Standing Advisory Commission on Human Rights
SDLP	Social Democratic and Labour Party of Northern Ireland, social democratic and nationalist party formed in 1970 from the merger of civil rights activists, labour activists and former members of the Nationalist Party and the National Democratic Party, led by John Hume MEP MP
SF	Sinn Féin ('ourselves'), republican political party with historical links to the IRA, led by Gerry Adams MP
STV	Single Transferable Vote
UDA	Ulster Defence Association, illegal loyalist paramilitary organisation, on cease-fire as this book went to press
UDP	Ulster Democratic Party, loyalist political party with historical links to the UDA, led by Gary McMichael
UDR	Ulster Defence Regiment, former regiment of the British Army recruited in Northern Ireland, with an almost exclusively Protestant composition
UFF	Ulster Freedom Fighters, loyalist paramilitary organisation, a component of the UDA

UKUP   United Kindom Unionist Party, led by Robert McCartney MP, an integrationist unionist party which supports the DUP in its opposition to the 1998 British–Irish Agreement

USC   Ulster Special Constabulary, known unofficially as the 'B Specials', former paramilitary police reserve, exclusively Protestant in composition

UUP   Ulster Unionist Party (also known as the Official Unionist Party [OUP]), governed Northern Ireland from 1920 until 1972, led by David Trimble MP, supporter of the 1998 British–Irish Agreement

UVF   Ulster Volunteer Force, illegal loyalist paramilitary organisation which takes its name from the body recruited to oppose Irish home rule in the early twentieth century

WP   Workers' Party, Marxist–Leninist party formed from SFWP, Sinn Féin the Workers' Party

Introduction

In 1998, after two years of formal negotiations, and after at least three years of pre-negotiations, eight political parties and two sovereign governments, aided by many third parties, agreed upon a political settlement designed to end nearly thirty years of political violence in Northern Ireland. The parties and governments argued, bargained, cajoled and confronted one another, but eventually agreed the sketch of a new constitutional order: an imaginative and novel order, subsequently endorsed in two referendums of citizens, held on the same day, in both parts of Ireland. The godly and the ungodly who supported the settlement call it the Good Friday Agreement, after the name of the day it was finally made.

The new order makes constitutional what was politically and socially true: it confirms that Northern Ireland is both British and Irish. It recognises two nationalities, British and Irish, and their local designations, unionist and nationalist. It recognises others who are neither nationalist nor unionist, nor British nor Irish – though perhaps both. It promises that legislative and executive power will be divided and shared in a devolved government. It promises the deployment of collective and co-operative political energy within the region, across the island of Ireland, above and across all these islands adjacent to northwestern Europe, and indeed within the European Union. It promises pluralism with justice, difference with equality, citizenship with nationality, politics with peace, legitimacy with law. It promises that local power will be held and shared proportionately. It promises Christians and the non-religious that they can school their children as they see fit with equal funding. It promises citizens the right to use their tongues, or the tongues of their ancestors, as they wish, in school or elsewhere. It promises legal and political protections, double protections, rights: rights to majorities and minorities; to the present unionist majority and the present nationalist minority; to the three minorities that loom on the immediate electoral horizon, of unionists, nationalists and others; and, beyond that horizon, to a possible new majority of nationalists, and a possible new minority of unionists.

The Good Friday Agreement is compelling if not miraculous architecture, a work of collective political art that rightly wins the admiration of political scientists and constitutional lawyers. In our professional argot it is a consociational agreement.

A consociation, that is, an association of societies (*con* derives from the Latin for 'with') is based on four principles: executive power-sharing, proportionality, community self-government, and minority veto rights. The Good Friday Agreement is also a confederal and federal agreement that shares sovereign powers and functions in complex and subtle ways. The Agreement has interests, identities, and ideas studded, but carefully poised and balanced, throughout all its complex political buildings. It appears to learn from the past to mend the present, and to allow a future without a politics of antagonism. It has brought the Nobel peace prize to a very small place.

And yet, as we write on 30 October 1998 we have a cold peace rather than a fully realised political settlement. Implementing the Agreement was always going to be at least as difficult as making it. Its makers, rightly, remain full of hope. Prisoners are leaving jails, army patrols are being scaled down, and politicians have been elected to office. A novel dual premiership is in existence – with a First Minister and Deputy First Minister who are equals in everything but their titles. British public law and Irish constitutional law have been processed to confirm the Agreement in domestic and international law. Certain just truths have been spoken, but reconciliation, in truth, has been limited. As we write, one political party insists that another must arrange the decommissioning of the weapons of its paramilitary associates before it may sit with its proportionate share of executive power in the new political order. The party that makes this insistence is weakened by internal faction. It seeks to bargain again for what it missed, or lost, on Good Friday. It bargains from weakness rather than new-found strength. The party it criticises resorts to legalism. It complains, correctly, that the Agreement required no prior decommissioning of weapons by it, or by its associates, before it could take its duly won share of executive seats. It agrees that decommissioning must happen within two years of the making of the Agreement, but adds, not just yet. It insists that the letter of the bargain is kept, being unable, it appears, to help its new political partner even if it understands its difficulties. We have, in short, a crisis of executive formation.

A crisis has three potential futures: it can be resolved; it can persist; it can terminate the entity experiencing it. By the time this book is published we will all know whether the crisis of executive formation has been resolved. It may have been resolved through cabinet formation and movement on decommissioning being accomplished on a single day. It may persist, freezing the promise of the Agreement without breaking it completely. Lastly, it may have plainly broken the full promises of the Agreement and the multiple informal coalitions upon which it rested. We hope that the crisis will have been resolved when this book is read, and we fear that it will persist. But if the crisis has terminated the Agreement we shall not plunge into despair: if that happens, something rather like the Agreement will have to be rebuilt, painstakingly, from the architecture of Good Friday.

The subject of our book, police reform, has the same potential as the present crisis of executive formation. It may terminate the Agreement, for now; it may freeze its progress; or it may confirm the breakthrough to a new political order. The late Frank Wright maintained that 'in national conflicts, law, order and justice are not issues that happen to arise from other causes. National conflicts, once they are fully developed, revolve around these matters.'[1]

Police reform in Northern Ireland is at the organisational heart of the national conflict between nationalists and unionists and republicans and loyalists. Police reform was such a heated subject in the making of the Agreement that it was decided to postpone it. It was decided that an Independent Commission on Policing should be established with terms of reference that are published in Appendix A to this short book. The Patten Commission as it is now known, after its Chair, must publish its proposals by the summer of 1999.

We have written this short essay in policy analysis and policy advocacy to provide at least one public set of benchmarks against which the proposals of the Patten Commission can be judged. We believe that the Patten Commission's conclusions will be judged, firstly and correctly, by whether they are wholly consistent with the terms of reference given in the Good Friday Agreement; secondly and equally importantly, by whether they address the national conflict that underlies and expresses itself in the controversies over policing; and, lastly, by whether they make proposals that will be constructive, feasible and durable. This book has the same objectives as the Patten Commission should have: to be consistent with the terms of reference and with the letter and spirit of the Good Friday Agreement; to address the national conflict in our homeland; and to see that its arguments are judged constructive, and that they assist in the making of feasible, durable and just policing policies. Whether it achieves these objectives is not for us to judge.

A note on terminology

The politics of Northern Ireland, as the locals know and visitors soon learn, is a terminological minefield. The glossary on pages xi–xiii shows how we have handled the major terminological controversies. There is one piece of warning on wording that is essential in evaluating the need for police reform, and in evaluating the argument of this book. We insist it is neither pedantic, nor perverse. The reader must distinguish Catholics from nationalists, and Protestants from unionists.

To demonstrate the force of this distinction, we shall express it here in an apparently paradoxical form. We submit that the RUC may not have particularly bad relations with Catholics; we maintain that the RUC may not become a more legitimate police force even if it recruits more Catholics – even if the RUC is more religiously impartial in its conduct, whether at senior level or at street level; and we claim that the problem of the RUC is not fundamentally a sectarian problem. By contrast, we maintain that the RUC has particularly bad relations with nationalists; we maintain that policing in Northern Ireland can become more legitimate if and only if nationalists, as well as unionists and others, are recruited to the police; and we maintain that the police will sustain any such new legitimacy if, and only if, they become nationally representative and nationally impartial in their conduct, whether at senior level or at street level; we claim, in short, that the problem of the RUC is fundamentally a national problem.

Making this distinction clear, and sticking to it, is essential for focused thinking. While most Catholics in Northern Ireland are also nationalists, not all are. The latter, namely Catholics who are not nationalists, are generally not the source of any resistance to the legitimacy of the RUC. In consequence police reforms, past, present and future, that simply focus on recruiting Catholics, or on religious impartiality, do not address the core question, the policing of a nationally divided region in which rival national and political allegiances are held by most of the population. Equally, arguments that defend the status quo by maintaining that some or many Catholics are happy with the RUC are irrelevant – even if they are entirely true, which can be questioned. They are irrelevant because the issue of police reform is not, at base, a religious issue. That at least is the argument that knits this book together. Readers must decide for themselves whether or not it is true.

1

A police that is not everyone's*

All great truths begin as blasphemies.

GEORGE BERNARD SHAW, *Annajanska*

Unfortunately, there has been no reliable research into why Catholics are not prepared to join the RUC.

POLICE AUTHORITY FOR NORTHERN IRELAND[1]

The participants believe it essential that policing structures and arrangements are such that the police service is professional, effective and efficient, fair and impartial, free from partisan political control; accountable, both under the rule of law for its actions and to the community it serves . . .

THE GOOD FRIDAY AGREEMENT, 1998

An overwhelming majority of unionists and Protestants support the RUC. Partisan unionists regard the RUC as their police, protectors of the Union. Other unionists, by contrast, sincerely regard the police as everyone's police. They are unionists of goodwill – committed to treating Catholics as equal citizens of the Union. They mostly think that the police already meet the requirements of the Good Friday Agreement. In their eyes the police are already professional; effective and efficient; fair and impartial; free from partisan political control; tough but fair; tough on terrorists, be they republicans or loyalists; and tough on criminals.

Partisan unionists should not be surprised if nationalists complain that the RUC is partial – that, after all, is how they see 'their police'. This chapter is therefore not directed at the views of such partisan unionists. Its target is those unionists of goodwill who see the police as generally impartial, professional and neutral – an outlook they share with a minority of Catholics. It is they who need to be persuaded that their understanding of the RUC is incorrect; that the RUC, as currently constituted, is not everyone's police, and therefore does not fulfil the requirements of the new agreement. The Patten Commission also needs to be persuaded of these propositions.

Official nationalist views of the RUC

The simplest way of establishing what northern nationalists think of the RUC is to hear and read what they say. Two political parties organise almost the entire nationalist vote in Northern Ireland: Sinn Féin and the Social Democratic and Labour Party (SDLP). Sinn Féin is the more hardline of the two nationalist parties. In its republican analysis the RUC is a unionist as well as a sectarian police force, an instrument of unionist domination, a participant in the conflict rather than a neutral law enforcement agency. Sinn Féin maintains that the RUC's members have been linked to the repression, torture and killing of nationalists, and it highlights the fact that RUC personnel have colluded with loyalist paramilitaries. The RUC, in the words of Sinn Féin's Alex Maskey, is 'totally unacceptable to the entire nationalist people'.[2] In Sinn Féin's analysis the RUC cannot be reformed, it must be disbanded. As one republican activist puts it, 'A reformed RUC would amount to nothing more than painting a smile on the face of a corpse ... A totally reconstructed police force within the existing state is a non-starter.'[3]

Nationalists in the SDLP use less forceful language – they, after all, have always been constitutionalists, committed to the expression of Irish national self-determination by consent, to achieving a unified or agreed Ireland, by consent, and to reforming Northern Ireland, by consent. The SDLP's elected officials often emphasise the enormous human price paid by police officers and their families during the violence of the last thirty years. That does not, however, mean that they are tacit supporters of the RUC. On the contrary, the SDLP's spokespersons also claim that the RUC is unacceptable to nationalists. They have done so consistently; none more so than Seamus Mallon MP, now Deputy First Minister of Northern Ireland, and for many years the party's spokesman on justice. The SDLP emphasises that the police are not representative. Catholics comprise over 40 per cent of Northern Ireland's population, but make up just 7.5 per cent of the RUC, and not all of these Catholics are local Catholics, let alone nationalists.[4] The SDLP does not demand the 'disbanding' of the police, but it does argue that policing issues cannot be resolved by 'minor adjustments to the status quo'.[5]

These views of Sinn Féin and the SDLP represent long-established policy positions, which the two parties regularly air in their manifestos, party literature, speeches and media interviews. Alex Maskey's perspective is as representative of Sinn Féin's as Seamus Mallon's is representative of the SDLP's. We have read through these two parties' literature for signs that these views are overstated, or reactions to specific crises or episodes, but have found no evidence to sustain such interpretations. On the contrary, they are typical. The official views of the two nationalist parties, which now average approximately 40 per cent of the vote between them in regional elections to the Westminster parliament, the Northern Ireland Assembly, the European Parliament, and local government districts, are utterly unambiguous: the RUC is unacceptable to nationalists. Moreover, the two nationalist parties do not believe that their official views lose them any votes, if we are to judge by the incredulous reactions of their spokespersons when this suggestion is put to them.

Responses to the official views of nationalists on the RUC

Many defenders of the status quo discount the unified nationalist rejection of the RUC. Unionists of goodwill often claim that 'many Catholics' or (less often) 'many nationalists' find the RUC acceptable, and that nationalist leaders exaggerate the degree of minority disgruntlement. They often concur with one key argument of partisan unionists, particularly voluble within the Democratic Unionist Party (DUP), but which is also expressed by people who do not regard themselves as partisan unionists. This argument is widely held within the Ulster Unionist Party (UUP), the United Kingdom Unionist Party (UKUP), the Conservative Party, the RUC and the Police Authority for Northern Ireland (PANI). It is short and simple: opposition to the RUC is primarily the result of republican terrorist intimidation.

During Westminster's parliamentary debate on the Police (Northern Ireland) Bill in December 1997, practically all unionist and Conservative speakers made this argument a central motif of their speeches. Robert McCartney MP of the UKUP maintains that 'there is such low recruitment from the minority community because its members are murdered, maimed and ostracized ... the criminal political element will not permit ordinary people to display their confidence in the RUC'.[6] Andrew Mackay MP, the Conservative Party's spokesperson on Northern Ireland, shares this verdict: 'Slogans about the RUC being unacceptable in nationalist areas will be vehemently rejected by the Opposition ... Today, the main obstacle for many is not necessarily the nature of the force, but the fear of intimidation from within the communities in which they live.'[7]

So, the argument of partisan unionists and of many unionists of goodwill is that the (Catholic or nationalist) minority refuses to embrace the RUC, or apply for membership, because of republican terrorism. The London *Times* complains that the RUC is even prevented from conducting road safety classes in Catholic schools because republicans block this anodyne activity.[8] Catholics do not join the police because that would mean endangering their lives and those of their relations, and would leave them unable to return to their communities.[9] Catholic officers have to send their children to Protestant schools and they and their relatives cannot attend their preferred places of worship because of security risks. In the RUC's *Fundamental Review of Policing*, released by it in summary form, 'intimidation' is the sole explanation offered for low numbers of Catholic police officers.[10] In evidence before the Northern Ireland

Affairs Committee, the Chief Constable maintained, more circumspectly, that intimidation was the 'major' reason preventing Catholic recruitment.[11] The RUC emphasises opinion polls in which Catholics give fear of intimidation as the most frequent reason for why co-Catholics refuse to join the RUC (see Table 1.1). The police also point out that Catholic applications to the RUC almost doubled in the year after the first IRA cease-fire – going from 11.7 per cent of applicants in 1993 to 20.3 per cent in 1995 – and note that they fell off (to 16 per cent) in 1996, after the IRA called off its cease-fire in February of that year.[12]

Sometimes, unionists of goodwill put the blame for the 'perception' that Catholics are alienated from the RUC on nationalist politicians, including SDLP officials, and on leaders of Catholic civil society, and Catholics' religious leaders. They suggest that Catholics do not join or embrace the RUC because they follow their leaders' instructions. When Sinn Féin and the SDLP refuse to attend meetings hosted by the Police Authority for Northern Ireland, or local

Table 1.1

Public opinion on why Catholics are deterred from joining the RUC, 1995–6

Q. Which, if any, of the reasons given do you think might deter Catholics from joining the police force in Northern Ireland?	PROTESTANTS %	CATHOLICS %	ALL %
Fear of intimidation or attack on them and their relatives	68	63	66
Fear they couldn't maintain contact with family and friends	51	53	52
Other Catholics put pressure on them not to join	55	44	51
Don't join because they don't support the system of government	33	30	32
They feel they would be treated badly in the police	13	22	16
They try to join, but are not chosen because of their political beliefs	7	14	10
They try to join, but are not chosen because of their religion	6	14	9
Other reasons	1	2	2
None of these	2	1	2

N (Total) = 4,798; Protestants = 2,959; Roman Catholics = 1,839

Source: Northern Ireland Affairs Committee, *Composition, Recruitment and Training of the RUC*, Vol. II, *Minutes of Evidence and Appendices* (London, Stationery Office, 1998), p. 21.

Community–Police Liaison Committees (CPLCs), they are accused of deliberately preventing Catholics from identifying with the RUC. The Gaelic Athletic Association (GAA) is also blamed because of its regulation, Rule 21, that no one can play Gaelic games while being a member of the UK's security forces. Gary McMichael, the leader of the loyalist Ulster Democratic Party (UDP), believes that 'the enforcement of Rule 21 is a distinct discouragement against Catholics joining the RUC ... One of the reasons why Catholics have been deterred from joining the RUC is because nationalism has made it unacceptable for Catholics to join.'[13]

Some academics think that the unacceptability of the RUC among Catholics is exaggerated. John Brewer, a sociologist at Queen's University Belfast, criticises what he describes as a 'divided society' model of policing.[14] This model suggests that the police reflect the divisions in Northern Ireland, with Protestants defending the police while Catholics attack them. Brewer claims, by contrast, that there are important 'intra-communal' fissures on policing which this 'divided society' model overlooks. His research suggests that not all Protestants like the police, but also that significant numbers of Catholics respect the RUC. Survey data, he believes, show that 'an appreciable number of Catholics and nationalists are not alienated from the RUC' and that 'Catholic attitudes towards the police are more positive and heterogeneous than has been presented in the past'.[15] Brewer's interpretation of survey data is consistent with fieldwork he has conducted with a colleague – they argue that RUC officers routinely distinguish between Catholics who are supportive of the police and those who are not.

There is plainly a deep polarisation here. Sinn Féin claims that the RUC is 'totally unacceptable' to nationalists, while the claim that the RUC has broad support across the two communities is used by unionists of goodwill to argue that substantive reforms of the RUC are not needed. Conor Cruise O'Brien takes a characteristically harder unionist line: he maintains that because opposition to the RUC springs mainly from IRA manipulation, implementing any reforms in effect constitutes appeasement – which would be not only wrong, but ultimately also either futile or, worse, perverse. In

O'Brien's opinion, the demand for reform is an orchestrated tactic to demoralise the RUC before a resumption of republicans' military campaign.[16] This logic is taken in further emotive directions by those who insist that substantially reforming the RUC would be a posthumous insult to those officers who have been killed during the last thirty years. Thus Nigel Dodds of the DUP writes:

> Any attempt to change the name of the RUC or to abolish the oath of allegiance to the Queen as a sop to republican demands will be fiercely resisted by unionists. Enough concessions have already been given to the IRA and their fellow travellers with nothing in return and such a move would be regarded as a betrayal of all those RUC officers who have died or been seriously injured over 25 years of troubles.[17]

When the Patten Commission was established, the *Daily Telegraph* published the photographs of officers who had been killed, no doubt intending the same inference to be drawn.

Unionists of goodwill generally suggest that what is really needed is not police reform but for Catholic and nationalist leaders to support the police, sit on the Police Authority, and encourage Catholics to become police officers. In their eyes the nationalist claim that the RUC, and the political agencies that oversee it, is largely composed of Protestants and unionists is a self-fulfilling prophecy, the responsibility of nationalists themselves. If only nationalists would participate in recruitment and in holding the RUC to account, they would gain the input they currently deny themselves.[18] Hardline unionists think the self-fulfilling prophecy is entirely conscious: nationalist politicians know that their failure to participate in police bodies or to encourage their followers to become police officers discredits the Union, and therefore advances the prospects of a united Ireland.

Lastly, a plausible claim is made by senior police officers and unionists of goodwill: what is desperately needed are permanent paramilitary cease-fires, an end to punishment beatings by paramilitaries, and a political settlement, and then the police will be broadly accepted in Northern Ireland. If there is no violence, there will be no need for the police to engage in counterinsurgency practices: the police could be 'normalised', they could revert to community policing, and to controlling ordinary crime; armoured Land Rovers could be replaced by the 'bobby on the beat'; and young Catholics who want to police would be able to join the RUC. As the Chief Constable puts it, the 'major' change needed is 'in the environment in which we operate'.[19] The London *Times* editorialises in the same vein, complete with a now characteristic Scottish reference: 'The RUC could become a normal police force tomorrow, in the same way as, say, the Lothian and Borders police are, if republicans were unequivocally to abandon the armed struggle and decommission their arms.'[20]

A political settlement would undoubtedly aid 'normalisation', though it is wrong to imply that Northern Ireland once had 'normal', that is, legitimate, impartial and professional, policing.[21] We agree that nationalists have been primarily discontented with Northern Ireland's constitutional arrangements, and therefore that the new political settlement creates an opportunity to establish legitimate, impartial and professional policing. But it is an error to forget that the new political settlement included promises of police reform – and these promises were critical ingredients in winning overwhelming endorsement for the Agreement among nationalist (and republican) voters in both parts of Ireland. It is another error to forget that discontent with the previous constitutional arrangements was based not just on their form, but also on their content and consequences – which included policing structures. Andrew Mackay believes that 'the establishment of political stability will do more than any institutional reform to attract more applicants from the nationalist community'.[22] This is a deeply misguided thesis. The new political settlement is premised upon police reform, and the prospect of political stability depends upon police reform.

Weighing the evidence

Hardline unionists oppose any significant reform of the RUC. Unionists of goodwill are not persuaded of its necessity, though they are prepared to acknowledge that there is some estrangement between the RUC and Catholics and nationalists, and are open to proposals for moderate reforms. This is the nub of potential conflict: unionists of goodwill and nationalists have agreed a political settlement, but they disagree over the scope of policing reform.

The role of the Patten Commission, and of professional policy analysts, must be to judge the competing evaluations of the necessity or otherwise of police reform. The view that nationalists find the RUC 'totally unacceptable' cannot be reconciled with the thesis that opposition to the RUC is confined to a small and intimidatory republican fringe. It is important, therefore, to obtain a reasonable assessment of Catholic and nationalist attitudes towards the RUC. It is also vitally important to distinguish Catholic from nationalist attitudes. Not all Catholics are nationalists, though nearly all nationalists come from cultural Catholic backgrounds. In consequence, survey or ethnographic data that focus on Catholics are likely to reveal a minority who are not nationalists and who are prepared to endorse the Union – for example, Catholic supporters of the Alliance Party. These Catholics are less likely, other things being equal, to have political and non-political problems with the RUC. The failure to make the distinction between Catholics and nationalists, we believe, leads some people to think with the wrong 'divided society' model. The primary local division is not between Protestants and Catholics but rather that between unionists and nationalists – though, of course, these divisions are highly correlated.

There is little doubt that violent republican intimidation deters Catholics from joining the RUC. Most Catholics and most nationalists agree with this fact, but it is misleading and erroneous to focus exclusively on this factor. The survey evidence given to a parliamentary committee by the RUC (see Table 1.1) shows that intimidation is the most frequent reason chosen by Catholic respondents from the options available, but there is no way of telling from the questions or responses how many Catholics consider it the sole or even their most important explanation of why Catholics do not join the RUC. The responses cannot tell us which Catholics are deterred by intimidation (for example nationalist Catholics or unionist Catholics). The survey does show that significant proportions of

Catholics pick reasons in addition to (or instead of) republican intimidation when explaining why Catholics do not join the police.
Thus 30 per cent list their opposition to the system of government;
22 per cent think they would be badly treated in the police; while 44
per cent list community 'pressure' as another reason (that is political
and social norms as opposed to intimidation).

These data suggest that Catholics have several reasons for not
joining the police. Reasonable people should conclude that these
other reasons are likely to be more salient among nationalist as opposed to non-nationalist Catholics. These considerations are also reinforced by fieldwork research conducted by several academics,
who would classify themselves as neither nationalist nor unionist.
For instance, a study of Belfast, Derry/Londonderry, and Dun-
gannon found that while intimidation mattered, 'the view persisted
among many Catholics that the RUC remained essentially a Protestant or unionist force'.[23] The Opsahl Commission, which examined Northern Ireland in 1992–3 and undertook extensive public
hearings, found that Catholic reluctance to enlist in the RUC was
'due less to fear of reprisal from the IRA and more because of the
nationalist perception of the RUC as the instrument of a state which is
still seen as British and unionist, and therefore as not "belonging" to
their community' (emphasis added).[24] Even the Police Authority,
which in the past has emphasised the role of intimidation, points
out in its latest annual report that Catholics also 'feel they may suffer
prejudice or have to submerge their cultural and religious background to "fit" within the RUC'.[25] Hardheaded realists may think
such reasoning is typical of liberal-minded people and social scienti-
fic researchers, but if so they have to address a simple question: how
did republican militants sustain themselves over thirty years and
carry out systematic attacks on police officers and army personnel
if the local population of Catholics and nationalists had no serious
difficulties with the RUC?

We might appear to have a chicken-and-egg research issue:
which came first, republican intimidation or nationalist hostility towards the police? The historical evidence may help dissolve this impression. Emphasising 'intimidation' as the primary explanation of

Catholic and nationalist dispositions towards the RUC is simply not historically convincing. Catholics have not joined the RUC in large numbers at any time, even when there was relatively little or no republican violence, and even when there were no effective republican organisations that could have successfully intimidated them. Before the most recent republican campaign began in 1969, the proportion of Catholic police officers was just a little over 10 per cent.[26] True, the proportion of Catholic applications to join the force increased to relatively high levels in 1995, the year after the first IRA cease-fire, but this level (20 per cent) is less than half of the Catholic share of the population, especially within the relevant age cohorts – and we have no way of knowing what proportion of these Catholics regard themselves as nationalists.[27] These low application levels have persisted despite two important facts: Catholic males are twice as likely to be unemployed as Protestant males, and police salaries are among the most lucrative available in Northern Ireland.

The argument that authentic Catholic and nationalist opposition to the police is restricted to a small violent minority is also contradicted by continuous opinion polling data, including that gathered by the Police Authority and by non-partisan academic sources. Of course, survey data in Northern Ireland, and in divided regions generally, have to be treated with multiple cautions. Surveys provide snapshots of opinion and may not produce reflective or considered responses. In the presence of ethnic or national strife, and the dangers associated with airing radical views to a stranger, especially about governmental or police officials, respondents may exaggerate their moderation or conventionality. This fact may explain why the Alliance Party often does much better, and Sinn Féin and the DUP much worse, in opinion polls than in elections.[28] A further caution is apposite: American sociologist Ronald Weitzer notes that 'support for various aspects of policing may be more shallow than affirmative responses suggest, even if there is a high degree of consistency across different polls'.[29]

Yet, despite these important reservations, survey data from Northern Ireland register strong levels of Catholic and nationalist disenchantment with the RUC. Here we focus on two issues:

(1) perceptions of police partiality among Catholics and nationalists; and (2) Catholic and nationalist views on whether the RUC should be reformed.

There is a widespread view among Catholics that the RUC is biased towards Protestants. This view has remained consistent throughout much of the last thirty years (see Table 1.2).[30] It is also reflected in all three 'community consultation' surveys undertaken by the Police Authority between 1996 and 1997 (Table 1.3). In the latest of these, one of the most favourable to the RUC, 29 per cent of Catholics thought the RUC treated both communities equally, but 55 per cent thought that Protestants were treated better. By contrast, whereas 13 per cent of Protestants thought that their community was treated better by the RUC, only 1 per cent of Catholics thought Catholics were so favoured. The data in Tables 1.2 and 1.3 are unambiguous: Catholics and nationalists have consistently regarded the police as partial towards Protestants. They additionally suggest that nationalist Catholics hold this conviction more than Alliance-supporting Catholics. They also confirm that considerable minorities of unionists believe that Catholics and nationalists are correct in their perceptions of police partiality.

The major division among Catholics on the subject of police reform is also clear: it is over whether the RUC should be reformed or replaced/disbanded, that is, Catholics are divided between the recommendations of the SDLP and those of Sinn Féin. These opinions are also not merely snapshots but reflections of durable attitudes. In the latest survey conducted by the Police Authority, 77 per cent of Catholics want the RUC either to be reformed (42 per cent) or to be replaced/disbanded (35 per cent), while less than one in five, 18 per cent, appear to want the status quo (see Table 1.4).

The survey questions in Table 1.4 cannot be used to establish what scale of change is sought by those Catholics who opt for reform rather than replacement/disbandment of the RUC, but other recent surveys shed some light on this issue. One conducted in December 1997 showed that 70 per cent of Catholics thought 'complete reform' of the police service was 'essential' to a lasting settlement, while a further 11 per cent thought it 'desirable'.[31] The

Table 1.2 (a)
Public opinion and the RUC, 1978

Q. *The RUC is doing its job well.*

	PROTESTANTS	CATHOLICS
Strongly agree	60.6	17.9
Moderately agree	27.0	33.6
Slightly agree/slightly disagree/moderately disagree/ strongly disagree	11.6	48.8

Source: Northern Ireland Attitudes Survey 1978, archival deposit at Essex University by Prof. Edward Moxon-Browne.
Notes: Figures in per cent, N = 1,205, missing observations 72 (5.6 per cent of 1,277), Catholics comprised just 32.4 per cent of respondents who gave answers. There were serious political and methodological difficulties with this survey as Prof. Moxon-Browne discusses in *Nation, Class and Creed in Northern Ireland* (Aldershot: Gower, 1983). We have presented the data in a manner that, despite its limitations, clarifies the strong disagreements between Protestants and Catholics.

Table 1.2 (b)
Public opinion and the RUC, 1985

Q. *The RUC discharges its duty very unfairly/unfairly/fairly/very fairly.*

The RUC discharges its duty	PROTESTANTS	CATHOLICS
Unfairly/very unfairly	4	53
Fairly	59	43
Very fairly	37	4

Source: Poll, *Belfast Telegraph*, 2 June 1985.
Note: All figures are in per cent.

second, conducted in May 1998, revealed that 60 per cent of Catholics were in favour of 'radical reform' for the RUC.[32] The message from these polls is clear: a decisive majority of Catholics are in favour of substantial changes to policing. (The polls also show that most Protestants want the police to stay the way they are now, and that there is almost no support for disbanding the RUC among Protestants.)

Catholic and nationalist concerns about the RUC are reflected in responses to other questions in polls and surveys. Data from

Table 1.2 (c)
Public opinion and the RUC, 1989–95

Q. Please use this card to say whether you think Catholics are treated better than Protestants in Northern Ireland, or whether Protestants are treated better than Catholics, or whether both are treated equally. [A range of subjects follow.] And the RUC – how do they treat Catholic and Protestant members of the public?

Year of survey	Protestants who think the RUC treat Protestants better than Catholics	Catholics who think the RUC treat Protestants better than Catholics
1989	13.2	51.8
1990	12.0	53.9
1991	17.7	47.7
1993	16.8	47.4
1995	14.4	48.2

Per cent of party supporters who think the RUC treat Protestants better than Catholics

Year	DUP	UUP	ALLIANCE	SDLP	SF
1989	19.6	8.8	33.3	57.1	95.5
1990	11.5	7.7	48.6	50.4	83.3
1991	12.5	15.5	35.6	48.0	93.5
1993	23.3	12.6	18.5	53.2	95.5
1995	13.8	14.7	24.5	49.5	79.5

Source: British and Northern Ireland Social Attitudes Surveys (1989–95).
Notes: (a) All figures are in per cent. (b) Non-religious, non-party identifiers and don't knows/refused are excluded. (c) The Sinn Féin sample is very small, and significantly under-reports the party's electoral support. (d) DUP supporters are generally more likely than other unionist respondents to regard the RUC as partial towards Protestants – 1991 was an exception. (e) Generally half of all SDLP supporters regard the RUC as partial towards Protestants whereas Sinn Féin supporters solidly hold this view.

October 1997 show that while 21 per cent of Catholics had 'a lot of confidence' (17 per cent) or 'total confidence' (4 per cent) in the police's ability to conduct public order policing impartially, 39 per cent of Catholics either had 'little confidence' (23 per cent) or 'no confidence at all' (16 per cent). From the RUC's perspective the figures improve somewhat when Catholics are asked to judge its ability to conduct ordinary day-to-day policing, with 29 per cent expressing a lot of confidence or total confidence, and 30 per cent

Table 1.3

Public opinion and the RUC's treatment of Protestants and Catholics, 1996–7

	PROTESTANTS			CATHOLICS		
	RCs better treated	treated equally	Ps better treated	Ps better treated	treated equally	RCs better treated
September 1996	7	71	15	67	26	1
February 1997	8	69	15	64	26	0
October 1997	7	70	13	55	29	1

Source: Police Authority for Northern Ireland, *Reflecting All Shades of Opinion* (Belfast: PANI, 1998), Table 10b, p. 11.
Note: Don't Knows/Refusals varied between 7 per cent and 9 per cent among Protestants, and between 7 per cent and 13 per cent among Catholics, and are excluded from the tables. The higher Catholic Refusal or Don't Know rate may be significant.

having little confidence or no confidence at all. Protestants are significantly more supportive of the RUC's ability to conduct both types of policing: 53 per cent expressed a lot of confidence or total confidence in the police's public order role, while 64 per cent expressed these sentiments about their ordinary policing role.[33]

This evidence suggests that Northern Ireland fits the model of a 'divided society' on policing rather well. In this model, the main axis of division of opinion takes place along ethnic or cultural boundaries rather than along some other axis such as age or class.[34] The data fit a unionist–nationalist division even better than they do a Protestant–Catholic division, but they fit both. Catholics are clearly much more likely to have problems with the police than Protestants. The late John Whyte, who was always scrupulous with data, pointed out that the two political communities are often more divided on security issues, like policing, than they are on constitutional matters.[35] Their recent support for the 1998 Agreement (albeit with near unanimity among nationalists and Catholics compared to an even split among Protestants and unionists) and their current polarisation on attitudes towards policing reform is entirely consistent with the pattern Whyte detected in the 1970s and 1980s. There are, of course, divisions within each national group on policing issues – there is, after all, seldom unanimity in

Table 1.4

Public opinion on the future of the RUC, 1995–7

PROTESTANTS

	RUC should be allowed to carry on exactly as now	RUC should be reformed	RUC should be replaced	RUC should be disbanded	Don't know/ Refused
1995	71	23	4	0	1
1996	61	32	4	0	2
1997 (Feb.)	68	26	4	0	2
1997 (Oct.)	70	25	3	0	24

CATHOLICS

	RUC should be allowed to carry on exactly as now	RUC should be reformed	RUC should be replaced	RUC should be disbanded	Don't know/ Refused
1995	28	38	31	1	2
1996	13	46	32	4	5
1997 (Feb.)	11	52	29	5	4
1997 (Oct.)	18	42	33	2	4

Source: Police Authority for Northern Ireland, *Reflecting All Shades of Opinion* (Belfast: PANI, 1998).

an ethnic, cultural or national group on any issue. What matters, however, is whether these internal disagreements are less important than those between the communities.

Not all Protestants endorse the RUC, perhaps particularly since its policing of anti-Anglo-Irish Agreement protests after 1985, and of controversial Orange parades since 1995. Fieldwork rather than opinion surveys shows that younger, working-class, urban Protestants are less likely to trust the police than other Protestants, and more likely to support changes to policing, albeit moderate changes. Loyalist politicians are also more likely to criticise police methods than mainstream unionist parties. This does not mean, however, that they favour significant constitutional and political change for the police in the way that nationalists and Catholics do. As Billy Hutchinson, one of the two Progressive Unionist Party (PUP) Assembly members, puts it, 'Loyalists support the police but are opposed to some police tactics.'[36]

Similar fieldwork suggests that middle-class and older Catholics are less likely to be hostile towards the police than other Catholics, and more likely to call for reform of policing rather than disbandment. The SDLP and its supporters are less critical of the RUC than Sinn Féin and its supporters. These intra-community divisions open up the possibility of designing some reforms acceptable to segments of both communities. This potential should not be exaggerated, however. The problem with any moderate package of reforms, designed to appeal to some Protestants and Catholics, is that it would be unlikely to satisfy the very sizeable proportion of Catholics who call for significant change.

Conclusion

The evidence from survey data shows that a significant majority of Catholics and nationalists are unhappy with current policing arrangements. It confirms what can be gleaned from in-depth interviews, or from analyses of the local papers read by Catholics and nationalists, or from listening to their representatives and community leaders in public and private. Catholics break down into a significant group of republicans who are fundamentally estranged from the RUC, have little or no confidence in it, and want to see it disbanded; another significant group that is unhappy with the police and wants substantial reforms; and a third and much smaller group that accepts the status quo. This evidence may not fit the claims of Sinn Féin that the RUC is 'totally unacceptable' to nationalists, but it is radically inconsistent with the claim that only a militant republican fringe genuinely oppose the RUC. The strength of nationalist opposition to the police suggests that while intimidation is a factor in explaining the low numbers of Catholic police officers, it is not the only and perhaps not the most important factor – it may be more a symptom than a root cause. To argue that Catholics will join the police if 'allowed' to do so by republican militants is, after all, to claim that Catholic youth are eager to join a force they think should be substantially reformed or even disbanded.[37]

Most Catholics and nationalists have very serious reservations about the RUC so we should not expect the maintenance and broadening of the paramilitary cease-fires on their own to result in a dramatic increase in the numbers of Catholics applying to become police officers, at least not to the levels where they would apply in proportion to their numbers of potentially qualified applicants. As nationalists are less estranged from the police in their 'ordinary policing' role compared to their 'public order role', it is reasonable to expect some peace dividend, some tacit legitimacy for the police among Catholics and nationalists. The RUC and its defenders are not wrong to talk about such a dividend, but it should not be relied upon, it should not be exaggerated, and limited tacit legitimacy should be carefully distinguished from authentic legitimacy.

The evidence firmly suggests that when nationalist political parties call for the police to be reformed or disbanded, or when nationalist civil society organisations such as the GAA operate sanctions against the police, they are reflecting the wishes of their followers rather than misrepresenting or manipulating them. The view that nationalists dislike the RUC because their leaders tell them to is not simply patronising, it is related to the view, expressed in many of the same sources, that nationalists' dislike of the Union is artificially fomented. We suspect this view is born of the same urges, the desire to wish away the claims for reform and the desire to deny the authenticity of nationalist sentiments. The fact is that nationalist and republican leaders are not free to endorse the existing RUC, or to encourage Catholics and nationalists to apply to join the RUC, or at liberty to take up seats on the Police Authority or local police liaison committees. The price of so doing would be a grave loss of credibility with their constituencies. When policing institutions are reformed in such a way that grassroots nationalists are able to identify with them, only then will nationalist leaders be able, and willing, to endorse the policing of Northern Ireland.

The establishment of power-sharing institutions and new

North–South institutions across the island of Ireland will undoubt-edly reduce nationalist political estrangement in Northern Ireland, and lead to nationalists' treatment as full political and national equals.[38] But even if they work smoothly and without major crises, it is doubtful that on their own they will lead nationalists, let alone republicans, to accept an unreformed RUC. Indeed, some survey evi-dence suggests policing reform is of more importance to more na-tionalists than was the promise of new political institutions.[39] In any case, nationalists regard policing reform as part of the overall settle-ment. Their representatives insisted in the negotiation of the Agree-ment that there be a commitment to policing reform as well as to new political institutions. The terms of reference of the Patten Commission reflect these concerns.

The same sources we have used to weigh this evidence confirm that while nationalists seek substantial policing reform as a mini-mum, most unionists are strongly against it. This evidence under-lines the difficulties faced by the Patten Commission, and the Westminster government. Policy analysts must therefore go be-yond confirming that changes to policing are authentically desired by nationalists and authentically opposed by unionists. We need to show how police reforms might be implemented in ways that are fair to unionists, nationalists and others, and that would respect their identities, interests and ideas.

2

Policing the enemy

the RUC's historical relationship
with northern nationalists

A body of persons employed to maintain civil order and investigate
breaches of the law.

'POLICE', definitional entry in *Basil Blackwell Encyclopaedia of Political Science*, 1991

Un-English beginnings

Police services emerge with the modern state and with industriali-
sation. In comparative perspective they have distinct histories and
an abundance of particular legal, political and managerial arrangements. We can, however, draw one simple comparative distinction
within the countries of Europe and the countries of European colo-
nisation. Those countries with legal institutions based on the common law have generally experienced the development of a police
accountable to the courts and comparatively decentralised in political accountability and their managerial structures. By contrast,
countries with Napoleonic legal and administrative systems,
though subject to the rule of law, have developed centralised policing forces and gendarmeries, or civil guards, under the direct
supervision of central governmental ministers. The history of policing in Ireland, North and South, in the nineteenth century had

most in common with the continental European pattern – a direct consequence of Britain's imperial and colonial relationship with Ireland.

Under the Act of Union, Ireland was not governed as if it were part of Britain: Ireland was centrally administered by a Lord Lieutenant, always a peer of the realm, and by a Chief Secretary and Under-Secretary, who were commoners. In the nineteenth century no Catholic was Lord Lieutenant or Chief Secretary and there were just two Catholic Under-Secretaries. Until the 1890s these imperial ministers governed through boards and other agencies that were not accountable to the Westminster parliament, let alone to Irish MPs. In effect they ran a prefecture in Ireland. The Poor Law and educational services were much more centralised than their counterparts in Great Britain. And so were the police.

Formal policing began in Ireland before it did in England. 'Peelers' in both jurisdictions took their name from Robert Peel, whose policing innovations in England were informed by his past office-holding. As Chief Secretary for Ireland in 1814 he had established the beginnings of a paid police force, and earned himself another reputation, as 'Orange Peel'. One historian of policing in Ireland puts the comparative history this way: 'Two entirely different police systems ... developed for a supposedly "united" kingdom. Britain got an unarmed policeman, answerable not to central government but to a watch committee and depending in the last analysis on the moral support of the community to enforce the law. Ireland, by contrast, got an armed garrison, rigidly disciplined and directly controlled by Dublin Castle, operating with the backing of the Martini-Carbine, the bayonet and the sword rather than the support of the community.'[1] Courtesy of British state-building efforts, Ireland under the latter part of the Union was policed through the Royal Irish Constabulary, the RIC, a name that emphasised its undemocratic and indeed unparliamentary character. Though it recruited large numbers of Catholics and Protestants, it was strongly disliked by Irish nationalists, and continuously attacked by militant republicans during Ireland's war of independence. It was the immediate predecessor of the Royal Ulster Constabulary.

A political as well as a conventional police, 1921–72

Northern Ireland came into existence after the UK's Government of Ireland Act of 1920. Its status was reinforced after its recognition in the Anglo-Irish Treaty of 1921, which gave the newly established Northern Ireland parliament the right to opt out of the formation of the Irish Free State. The partition of Ireland was opposed by all nationalists, who argued it denied the Irish people their right of national self-determination: it was carried out by the Westminster parliament without the express sanction of a single Irish MP, unionist or nationalist; and its execution was plainly at odds with the opinion of the majority of Irish people who had voted in the 1918 Westminster general election.[2] Hardline nationalists, republicans, opposed both partition and the Treaty. Softline nationalists opposed partition but looked forward to a future boundary commission, promised in the Treaty, which they thought would inevitably lead to proposals for the major reconstruction of Northern Ireland's borders – proposals that they hoped would make it 'unviable'. They also looked forward to another promise in the Treaty, the creation of a Council of Ireland to link them to their co-nationals in independent Ireland. Both hopes were to be dashed by 1925.

Northern Ireland was, to put it mildly, a surprising creation. It was formed against the historical desires of Irish unionists, who had wanted all of Ireland to remain within the Act of Union. For them, it was a second-best resolution of their conflict with Irish nationalists. Northern Ireland was also formed against the express wishes of Irish nationalists, North and South, and nationalists comprised about one third of the electorate of the new entity. It was not expected to last, not least because of the promised boundary commission.

The Ulster Unionist Party, the UUP, which would govern Northern Ireland from 1921 until 1972, ensured that Northern Ireland would survive much longer than either its supporters or its opponents expected. The party developed an internal strategy to unify Protestants and unionists and to disorganise northern nationalists, and an external strategy to prevent British and Irish intergovernmental co-operation that might damage their new political regime. Avoiding a significant boundary revision was a successful component of these strategies; so was the formation of the Royal Ulster Constabulary.

The RUC was formally established in June 1922. From its inception it was not simply charged with ordinary policing duties. The Westminster parliament devolved responsibility for internal security to the new parliament in Belfast, and so the RUC was given the job of defending the Union against all types of nationalist. This fact helps to explain why in the 1920s there were more than four times as many police officers per capita in Northern Ireland as there were in England or Scotland.[3] From the outset, the RUC was armed and paramilitary in character, unlike police forces in Great Britain, or even the new police in the Irish Free State – which also were formed in a civil war, but had the advantage of being legitimate in the eyes of most of the people they policed.

To assist it, the RUC was equipped with some of the most draconian police powers ever passed in a liberal democracy. These were contained in the Civil Authorities (Special Powers) Act of 1922, renewed annually until 1928, then for five years until 1933, and then made permanent. The act gave the government the right to intern people without trial – which it did between 1922 and 1925, between 1938 and 1946, and between 1956 and 1961 – to arrest people without warrants, to issue curfews, and to prohibit inquests. It included two notorious catchall clauses that allowed the government to use the act's sweeping powers in any possible scenario.[4] Other laws, notably the Public Order Act (1951) and the Flags and Emblems Act (1954), enabled the government to control non-violent forms of political opposition, and effectively outlawed the public symbolic display of nationalist allegiance among the minority population.

The RUC contravened the standard norm in legitimate liberal democracies that the police exercise a semi-autonomous or arm's-length relationship with civil and political authorities. Its senior officers were subordinate in practice to the political direction of the Northern Ireland government. From 1921 until 1972 one party, the UUP, composed the entire cabinet – with the exception of one ministerial appointment in 1969, its cabinets were exclusively composed of Protestants; and between 1921 and 1969, 93 per cent of the party's Stormont MPs were members of the Orange Order at the time of their election. It would be astonishing if any police service could have preserved its autonomy from political interference given this level of political monopoly and continuity. The RUC was closely supervised in particular by the Ministry of Home Affairs, whose top officials, according to one source, were 'strident defenders of Protestant interests and whose policies with regard to law and order were sometimes purely political and biased against Catholics'.[5]

This lack of police autonomy was condemned by the London-based National Council for Civil Liberties in a 1936 report. The report had little impact, as was apparent when the first Labour politicians to intervene in Northern Ireland thirty-three years later declared themselves 'stunned' by the lack of police independence from the ruling UUP. As Roland Moyle, parliamentary private secretary to James Callaghan in 1969–70, recalled, 'The way the old Home Affairs department in Northern Ireland ran the police, my God, I mean the police were the creatures of the mini-aristocracy.'[6]

This political direction and lack of autonomy of the police may not have been the intention of any individual police officers, though plainly most worked these arrangements without complaint. Inevitably, the initial political and military environment affected the nature and the internal make-up of the force, at all ranks. Even before the formation of Northern Ireland, key unionist leaders had built a state-in-waiting, an administration backed by a body of armed men. A provisional government, with a paramilitary organisation supplied through illegal gun-running, had been organised before the outbreak of World War One. A second arming of Protestants and unionists in the form of the Ulster Special Constabulary, the USC, took place from 1920 onwards under the supervision of Dawson Bates, who became Minister of Home Affairs in the first Northern Ireland cabinet. Its core membership of 5,500 full-time

A Specials was recruited from the Ulster Volunteer Force, the pre-war paramilitary organisation that had subsequently fought as a unit in the British Army during World War One. The A Specials were backed by 19,000 part-time B Specials, who together with the RUC were used to repress IRA actions in Northern Ireland during the 1920s. The Specials were exclusively Protestant, and regularly inti-midated Catholics and nationalists; their nature inevitably had an impact upon the regular police.[7] Moderate nationalist politicians drew distinctions between the Specials and the RUC, but the latter was inevitably tainted in nationalist eyes, especially given the fact that a significant proportion of the ranks of the RUC (around half in 1923 and one third in 1951) were ex-Specials.[8] Religiously, na-tionally and ethnically imbalanced policing was reinforced by the development of institutional affiliations between police units and Orange lodges. While RIC constables had been banned from mem-bership in the Orange Order, the UUP government lifted the ban for members of the RUC in 1922, and a police lodge was formed in 1923.

The historical record suggests, rather unconvincingly, that the RUC might have got off to a more balanced beginning. A commit-tee established in 1922 to organise the new police recommended, perhaps surprisingly, that it be representative of the population, that one third be Catholics, drawn in part from the ranks of the RIC.[9] However, proportionality never materialised. Catholic representa-tion peaked at 21 per cent of the RUC in 1923, and fell to 17 per cent by 1927, and to 10 per cent by the outbreak of the present round of conflict in 1969.[10] Nationalists did not apply to fill the official target for a number of reasons, including opposition to the state, fear of intimidation, and fear of ostracism from their own community.[11] There was also considerable unionist pressure on the government to ignore the committee's recommendation, and no serious attempt was made to recruit Catholics. Ministers simply argued, as we have seen that unionists of goodwill still do, that the blame for low num-bers of Catholics lay with nationalist leaders, who failed to encour-age Catholics to apply.[12]

Low Catholic representation, the Orange presence, the existence

of the Specials, and inter-recruitment between the Specials and the
RUC, all reinforced the impression among Catholics that the police
were, as a group of academics described them in the late 1980s, 'the
armed wing of unionism'.[13] They were seen as the successors of the
RIC, but subject to the more overt partisan influences of local unionism. The one-sided composition of the force also contributed to an
internal unionist culture that would act as a further barrier to the
future recruitment of Catholics.

For much of the period between 1921 and 1968, unionists exercised effective control over the minority population.[14] During the
periods of quiescence when the IRA was ineffective or not engaged
in campaigns, and when the RUC was confined to ordinary policing
duties, interactions between the police and Catholics could often be
civil. Relations deteriorated during periods of political unrest, however, when the combination of partisan control, emergency
powers, and Protestant personnel produced inevitable antagonisms.
Nationalists' protests were heavily policed, while loyalist counter-
protests 'rarely elicited any response'.[15] The inquiry by the National
Council for Civil Liberties in 1936 accurately found that the police
did not 'act impartially' but showed 'favouritism' towards Orange
mobs and tolerated attacks on Catholics. Nor was it always a question of the police reacting to nationalist protests. These protests
could themselves originate in response to police actions, as they did
during the 1950s when the RUC, acting under legislation recently
passed by the Stormont parliament, removed Irish Tricolours being
flown in predominantly Catholic and nationalist districts.

The partiality of the RUC and the Specials and protests about that
partiality are widely regarded as having been a significant factor in
the events precipitating the current conflict. When civil rights
marchers in October 1968 refused to be cowed by an order from
the Minister of Home Affairs to keep within Catholic areas of
Derry/Londonderry, tensions escalated. The RUC then ran amok
and attacked demonstrators in front of television cameras. On another occasion, in January 1969, marchers being escorted by the
police were ambushed at Burntollet bridge by a loyalist mob –
which included members of the RUC. Most seriously, the RUC and

Specials clashed with Catholic protesters in Derry/Londonderry in August of the same year, and subsequently invaded and damaged persons and property in what became known as the Battle of the Bogside.

These events, shown around the world by television, helped set the stage for Westminster's intervention in Northern Ireland in 1969. British troops were introduced not just because the RUC looked unable to control nationalist protests and a looming loyalist backlash, but also because it was certainly unable to do this impartially. The RUC's handling of the protests led to a number of reports which criticised the police's actions. The Cameron Commission, appointed to examine the outbreak of disturbances in late 1968, described a 'breakdown of [police] discipline', police involvement in the assault of civilians, and the use of provocative sectarian and political slogans by police officers. Both the Cameron Commission and the Scarman Tribunal, while stressing that the majority of police officers had acted professionally, found the police to be seriously at fault on several occasions.[16]

The predictable result of these events was the deepening of nationalist estrangement from the RUC. One reason why British troops were welcomed, at least initially, in predominantly nationalist areas, was that they were considered more capable than the police of protecting these communities impartially. Police behaviour during this period, according to one academic, 'remains vividly inscribed in people's memories and continues to influence perceptions of the police today',[17] a report which tallies well with our experiences in interviewing republicans and moderate nationalists.

Another result of these events was police reform. An inquiry by two senior police officers, Robert Mark and Douglas Osmond, and an investigation by a committee under Lord Hunt, both in 1969, were critical of the system of policing, particularly its paramilitary image and character, and its security role. Partly in response, between 1969 and 1973 a number of reforms were undertaken. These were collectively aimed at introducing into Northern Ireland what was seen as a British liberal model of policing, that is, an impartial police force which would be primarily responsible for 'normal' policing rather than paramilitary or political security duties. The reforms aimed at demilitarising, professionalising and depoliticising the police. The police were disarmed although they were soon rearmed, in early 1971, because of a deteriorating security situation and after the IRA launched its most vigorous offensive. The Civil Authorities (Special Powers) Act was repealed in 1973, a key demand of the civil rights movement. The Inspector-General of the RUC was given the less martial title of Chief Constable, in line with British practice. To promote non-sectarianism, the USC was disbanded, and its duties were undertaken by a new RUC reserve force and by the UDR, a locally recruited regiment under the command of the British Army GOC (NI). A Community Relations Branch of the RUC was established, and training programmes were developed to inculcate in recruits the need for neutrality between the two communities. To depoliticise the police, the Police Act (Northern Ireland) of 1970 created an independent Police Authority for Northern Ireland, also in line with British practice. Its role was to increase police accountability to the public, and to loosen the relationship between the RUC and the unionist Ministry of Home Affairs. It was stipulated that the Police Authority, unlike the government, would have to be 'representative' of the population. The process of removing the UUP's control over policing was taken even further in 1972, when the Stormont parliament was prorogued and the British government assumed direct responsibility for policing.

The RUC under British supervision, 1972–98

These reforms to the RUC, as well as subsequent, mostly minor, reforms, were not without consequence. Academic and other accounts of the police note a significant improvement in the quality of policing from the 1970s.[18] Party political depoliticisation was particularly successful. The UUP's control over policing was ended, and the RUC's leadership increasingly prided itself on its belief that it was above politics. By the end of the 1980s, the Chief Constable,

Jack Hermon, was refusing even to meet with unionist politicians lest it appear to compromise the police's neutrality. There were also advances in professionalism, the code word for impartiality. While the pre-1969 police had shown little enthusiasm for tackling loyalist protests, the RUC came to demonstrate considerable effectiveness in policing loyalist protests against the Anglo-Irish Agreement of 1985 and against the rerouting of Orange parades away from predominantly nationalist districts after 1996. One consequence of this greater impartiality was that police officers and their families were petrol-bombed from their homes in some predominantly Protestant districts during the anti-Anglo-Irish Agreement protests, and again in the mid-1990s. One officer was killed by a loyalist mob in Ballymoney in 1997, and another died from injuries suffered during an Orange Order protest in Portadown in 1998. Moreover, by the mid-1990s, the RUC could also point to impressive mop-up rates against loyalist paramilitaries. Between January 1994 and February 1998, 2,372 loyalists were arrested compared to 1,463 republicans, and 42 loyalists were charged with murder compared with 24 republicans.[19]

These changes, however, while they have earned the police some animosity from loyalists, particularly of the Orange Order persuasion, have not succeeded in their crucial aim of winning them legitimacy among nationalists. Instead, by the 1990s, as some wags put it, the police were merely considered 'equal-opportunity harassers'. As we saw in Chapter 1, a very solid majority of Catholics continue to believe that the police treat Protestants better than Catholics. The moderate nationalists in the SDLP have continued to refuse to sit on the Police Authority, to attend meetings with it, or to recommend to Catholics that they join up. Republicans continue to call for the force to be disbanded and, until recently, condoned the killing of police officers. Even the Northern Ireland Committee of the Irish Congress of Trade Unions, a non-aligned group, has not had sufficient confidence to take its seat on the Police Authority, and the police continue to come in for consistent criticism from other non-aligned groups, such as the Committee for the Administration of Justice.

The limits to reforming the RUC

Why did the RUC fail to win support from nationalists after the 1970s, despite apparently extensive and significant reforms? Two fundamental and related reasons immediately suggest themselves. One stemmed from the lack of a political agreement on the constitutional arrangements for the region, and the other from the presence of violent conflict and its consequences.

The reforms took place in the context of a continuing fundamental disagreement on the legitimacy of Northern Ireland. The thinking behind the reforms was based on the liberal premise that discriminatory policing was at the heart of the conflict, and that impartial enforcement of law and order was the cure. This reasoning ignored the fact that Northern Ireland's nationalist community aspired not merely to equal treatment before the law, like US blacks, but to an entirely different political dispensation, preferably one with different borders. They were Irish nationalists after all, and not British civic integrationists. Even if the reforms broke the RUC's links with the UUP regime at Stormont, they did nothing to sever its association with the Union. Nationalists and their leaders were not, in the absence of a settlement, prepared to concede legitimacy to even a reformed RUC, as they continued to reject the state it represented. This suggests that nationalist acceptance of the police in Northern Ireland requires not only police reforms, but a political settlement acceptable to nationalists.[20] However, even a settlement, such as the one so recently forged, does not mean that the RUC is acceptable to nationalists.

The reforms also took place in the context of an increasingly violent struggle between republican paramilitaries and the security forces. This had several damaging consequences for police–nationalist relations. First, it meant that even if the law was enforced wholly 'impartially' it would still be enforced disproportionately on nationalists, as they were more likely to challenge the state's laws, and to generate republican paramilitaries. Nationalists were disproportionately searched, arrested and convicted. Catholics were disproportionately the victims of plastic bullets fired by both the

British Army and the RUC. While internment operated with police and army arrests between 1971 and 1975, 2,060 republicans were detained compared to 109 loyalists.[21] In the period between 1969 and 1989, while the security forces – the British Army, the UDR and the RUC – killed far fewer republican paramilitaries (123) than numbers of their own were killed by republicans (847), they killed almost ten times as many republican paramilitaries as loyalist paramilitaries (13), and almost six times as many Catholic civilians (149) as Protestant civilians (25).[22] Had the RUC been flawlessly professional, this differential impact of the security forces on the Catholic population would nevertheless have adversely affected their relations with nationalists.

The violence of the 1970s also prompted security-minded, rather than reform-minded, responses from the authorities. Some reforms were more modest than they otherwise might have been, while others had to be abandoned altogether. Although the USC was disbanded, the UK government reincarnated it in the form of the Ulster Defence Regiment (UDR), a locally recruited branch of the British Army, only to have to abolish it later as it deservedly acquired the same stigma as the B Specials. A new RUC Reserve was also created. Moreover, in response to the conflict, the size of the local security establishment expanded. Manpower doubled between 1969 and 1972 alone (from 3,044 regular police in 1969 to 4,256 regular and 2,134 Reserve officers in 1972).[23]

While the Special Powers Act was repealed in 1973, the UK government created a new array of repressive security measures. The Special Powers Act was replaced by the Emergency Provisions Act 1973, which contained many of the same abuses as its predecessor, including the power of internment. It suspended the right to a jury trial for certain indictable offences, provided for new relaxed rules on the admissibility of evidence and on the onus of proof, and gave wider powers of arrest to the security forces. Up to half of the new act was directly inspired by the older legislation. It was soon buttressed by the Prevention of Terrorism Act, passed in 1974.[24]

The security situation also led the UK government eventually to resume using the police in a public order and indeed militaristic role in predominantly nationalist areas. The RUC was rearmed and re-militarised within a few months of having been disarmed. Increasingly, police barracks were permanently fortified. From 1971 until 1976 the RUC played a subordinate role to the British Army in security policy and action, but then the British government introduced a policy of 'police primacy' as part of a strategy of 'Ulsterisation' and 'normalisation' in which the RUC took on the leadership role in combating the IRA, although the British Army remained in a back-up position. The government was anxious that its role in Northern Ireland should be externally regarded as impartial and legitimate, and it may also have been anxious to reduce losses of army personnel. It was thought that the British Army's vanguard position made it easier for the IRA to argue it was involved in a war of liberation against a foreign army, and that this argument would be more ideologically difficult to advance if the IRA confronted a local police force. The RUC therefore underwent another significant expansion after 1976, comprising 7,700 regulars and 4,800 reservists by 1982.[25]

Police primacy was accompanied by a policy of 'criminalisation', aimed at demonstrating that those engaged in paramilitary activities were merely criminals rather than political activists. The success of this policy was entirely dependent on the government being seen to be relying on normal legal processes. It continued, however, to rely on the juryless (Diplock) courts and the extraordinary powers of arrest it had granted to all the security forces under the 1973 legislation, and to derogate from the European Convention on Human Rights on the grounds that there was an emergency. When internment without trial was abandoned, there was a corresponding increased reliance on confessions, extracted by the RUC using dubious, to say the least, 'questioning' techniques on arrested suspects.[26] Criticism by Amnesty International and the government-appointed Bennett Committee resulted in an embarrassed Westminster government placing new controls on police conduct.[27] But in consequence, however, confessions were replaced by accomplice evidence as the key method of securing convictions in the face of politically disciplined paramilitaries. By the early 1980s the RUC had cultivated the 'supergrass', a paramilitary who would implicate large numbers of his erstwhile colleagues in return for a new identity, relocation and substantial remuneration.[28] When 15 out of 25 supergrasses subsequently retracted their evidence (which led to the abandonment of this policing technique), it did nothing for Catholics' or nationalists' impression of the police or the judicial system in general – although in fairness one must observe that the RUC produced loyalist as well as republican supergrasses.

There were also compelling allegations of a 'shoot to kill' policy practised by special units of the RUC against republican paramilitaries in the early 1980s. Although an inquiry into these allegations produced evidence of a conspiracy to pervert the course of justice, the British Attorney-General, Sir Patrick Mayhew, decided in 1988 that it would not be 'in the national interest' to prosecute certain RUC officers.[29] In August and September 1989, evidence that the files of IRA suspects had been given to loyalist paramilitaries who used them to carry out murders raised questions about the partiality of both the UDR and the RUC. Nationalists were also antagonised by the RUC's role in forcing Orange parades through certain districts in the 1990s, particularly the Garvaghy Road in July 1996, and it does not seem to have helped its reputation that the RUC has also been willing to confront unionists and loyalists protesting against the re-routing of such parades. For most nationalists the unfinished story of the murder of Robert Hamill exemplifies the reality of the RUC's relationships with their community: a tale, at best, of cowardly indifference on the part of police officers, and, at worst, of collusion in a sectarian atrocity, corruption of due legal process, and cover-up of a homicide (see page 39). In addition to these particular episodes, and despite 'normalisation', in nationalist areas the RUC continued to rely on military-style snatch operations and a counterinsurgency style of policing.

The perception among many nationalists that the RUC, despite its senior officers' professions about their impartiality and professionalism, remained a biased force was compounded by the continuing overwhelmingly Protestant composition of the police, and by the

The Unfinished Story of Robert Hamill

Robert Hamill, a Catholic man, was kicked unconscious by loyalist youths as he walked home with a cousin and two women from St Patrick's Catholic Social Club in Portadown in May 1997. He died in hospital two days later. RUC officers in a nearby Land Rover witnessed the brutal attack. They did nothing. Hamill's sister Diane pointed out: 'Immediately afterwards the RUC issued three conflicting statements about this devastating event. But we know the truth and so do they. On that night we were given a frightening message. The life of someone like Robert Hamill in Portadown is worth nothing and is certainly not worth protection.' On 31 October 1997 the Northern Ireland Director of Public Prosecutions dropped charges against three of the six men accused of Hamill's murder. The Resident Magistrate was told that the charges were being dropped because the RUC could no longer rely on the evidence of certain witnesses. Hamill's family, according to their solicitor, will pursue private prosecutions against the released men. The solicitor has said, 'This incident was witnessed by a number of police personnel . . . No effort was made by police to prevent the incident or to apprehend any of the persons involved. It is surprising that though there were police there they can't supply evidence relating to this matter.' A spokesperson for the Committee for the Administration of Justice remarked, 'We remain puzzled as to why the police officers involved in this case do not appear to have been suspended pending the outcome of the inquiry.'

Sources: Irish Times, Dublin, 14 May, 1 November, 4 November and 5 November 1997.

---

fact that it was still possible, despite the criticisms contained in the Hunt Report, to be in the police and the Orange Order simultaneously. The Catholic proportion of police officers declined, in fact, from just over 10 per cent at the beginning of the Troubles to 7.5 per cent in 1997, during a period in which the number of officers more than doubled.

Partial recruitment was compounded by unsatisfactory arrangements for holding the police to account. The accountability structures devised in the 1969–72 period, and revised from time to time, were not sufficiently robust to satisfy nationalists, most Catholics, and liberal-minded unionists. The Police Authority, given limited powers to begin with, did not seem willing, in the face of the campaign of violence, to say anything remotely critical of the police, or to suggest a change of policy. As a result, even moderate nationalists, and trade union representatives, found it impossible to take their places. Local Community–Police Liaison Committees (CPLCs), established in the 1980s without a statutory basis, were also seen as ineffective talking shops, able to deal only with policing matters without a security dimension. They also failed to attract representatives of the nationalist community. Nor did a series of institutions responsible for overseeing complaints inspire confidence, since they failed to secure disciplinary action against officers in all but an extremely small proportion of complaints. A Police Complaints Board, established in 1977, was replaced by an Independent Commission for Police Complaints in 1988. The combination of reliance on emergency powers and the failure of civic accountability mechanisms prompted one commentator to ask if the RUC were in fact a 'law unto themselves'.[30]

The conflict in general, and normalisation in particular, had other negative effects. Not only did contact in violent and public-order situations increase nationalist estrangement from the police, it also did little for police attitudes towards nationalists. The police and the UDR, rather than British soldiers, became the main targets of republican militants after the adoption of Ulsterisation. Fear and animosity on the part of police officers reduced the likelihood of a gentle policing touch in predominantly nationalist areas. The deaths of police officers also made it more difficult for the British government or unionists to contemplate substantial reforms to policing, or for unionists to compromise with nationalists on policing, or anything else. Defenders of the status quo were able to argue that reforms to policing while republican gunmen were killing police officers was too much like appeasement to be considered as a serious option. They added that reforms would jeopardise the morale of a force that the British government had put in the front line of maintaining order.[31] These arguments were in line with the thinking of the Conservative government (in power from 1979 to 1997) on matters of law and order. The views of civil libertarians, like the Committee for the Administration of Justice, who maintained that the lack of radical police reform played into the hands of republican paramilitaries and fuelled the conflict, were ignored.

Conclusion: a new opportunity

This brief review of the history of the RUC's relations with northern nationalists suggests that the absence of police legitimacy has been importantly connected with the absence of political legitimacy for Northern Ireland: nationalists have found the RUC unacceptable because it has been associated with and has defended unacceptable political arrangements, as was true of its precursor, the RIC. In fact, northern nationalists have never been policed by services they regard as legitimate. This history suggests that a political settlement is a necessary condition if there are to be police services that are acceptable to northern nationalists. This does not mean, however, that a political settlement is a sufficient condition for northern nationalists to accept the police. Rather, many nationalists regard the police, because of the way they have interacted with them since 1921, and more particularly since 1969, as part of an unacceptable political system which needs to be changed. It is also their understanding that their politicians are signatories to an agreement that accepts this reasoning.

Review of the period since 1969 also suggests that violent conflict has erected tremendous obstacles to potentially worthwhile policing reforms. On the one hand, conflict produced a heavy-handed security response that estranged nationalists further from the RUC. On the other, violence from republican paramilitaries made it more difficult for the UK government and for moderate unionists to make concessions on policing reforms than might otherwise have been the case.

Fortunately, these two obstacles to constructing broadly acceptable police arrangements have been significantly eroded as a result of recent political developments. On Good Friday, 1998, eight of Northern Ireland's most significant political parties, and the British and Irish governments, reached a comprehensive political agreement, that included a commitment to policing reform (see

Appendix A). All major paramilitary organisations in the region are sustaining cease-fires as this book goes to press, and their political representatives who have significant electoral support, over 20 per cent of the electorate between them all, are committed to seeking political changes through exclusively democratic and peaceful methods. The legacy of the conflict is still relevant, and is still reflected in the continuation of polarised attitudes on policing reform, but there is now an unprecedented opportunity to build a police service acceptable throughout the communities of nationalists, unionists and others. The rest of this book offers our view on how this should be achieved.

3

Who should be in the police?

Security chiefs are expected to continue scaling down security measures in the coming weeks, but the peace process has left the RUC with a major dilemma over the building of new police stations, including one in Ballygawley, Co. Tyrone which was destroyed by an IRA bomb in December 1985 when two officers were shot dead. Plans were drawn up for work on the £1.7 million base to begin sometime next year but with the cease-fires in place, a decision has still to be taken to definitely go ahead. If they do, the authorities then have to decide if it should have the same anti-terrorist defences of other stations specially constructed to withstand gun, bomb and rocket attacks. New stations for Coleraine, Co. Londonderry and Ballymoney in neighbouring north Antrim are planned as well as part of a 10-year programme of priority development. Sinn Féin has objected to the proposed station in Ballygawley, a predominantly Catholic and nationalist town, but senior security advisers insisted tonight that political interference was not to blame for the delay in work getting under way. [A spokesperson] said: 'The changing situation has meant all sorts of new considerations having to be taken into account. Are some of these stations needed any more, and with the diminishing security threat what standard of protection should they have?'

Item on Press Association wires, 10 October 1998

The story in the above item from the Press Association's wires is typical of many that we have read in the last three years. It encapsulates some of the difficulties that the public and policy-makers face in considering the reform of the police. The RUC has lost many officers at the hands of the IRA and that has naturally made it and its supporters fearful and hostile towards paramilitaries, especially republican paramilitaries. Many nationalists nevertheless remain equally fearful of and hostile towards the presence of RUC barracks, or RUC patrols, and these sentiments are most intensely felt in predominantly republican areas. The UK government's security advisers, and the minister of state with special responsibility for security in Northern Ireland, Adam Ingram MP, just do not know whether they should rebuild destroyed barracks – to be prepared for any major breakdowns in the paramilitaries' cease-fires – or whether they should radically scale down their building commitments – in preparation for a long and, with luck, permanent peace. And, if they do decide that new police stations are necessary, irrespective of the 'security assessments' they receive, policy-makers do not know what they should look like, or where they should be located. Should they be war-proof fortresses, or neighbourhood drop-in centres? Should they be built openly and accessibly in predominantly nationalist areas as a confident investment in a new era of cross-community co-operation, or should they be built in more secure and militarily critical locations, as deterrents to any future generation of would-be republican militants?

The difficulties of police reform are therefore multiple, and complex. They are not, however, intractable. The core difficulties can be addressed by four succinct 'who, what and where' questions:[1]

- Who should be in the police?
- What kind of policing should Northern Ireland have?
- Where should the boundaries of policing units be drawn?
- What mechanisms should be used to hold the police to account?

This chapter addresses the first question. Its issue is the composition of the police.

Who should be in the police?

Our answer to this question is simple but in two parts: the police should be representative, and there should be just enough of them.

The police should, as far as possible, be representative of all the minorities in Northern Ireland: unionists (of the 'yes' and 'no' persuasions), nationalists and others; and of Protestants, Catholics, agnostics, atheists and those of other religious faiths; and of the majority as well as the minority in Northern Ireland, that is, women and men.

Above all, the police must be nationally representative. This criterion is the most important benchmark for change. The police should be representative of the region's diverse religious believers and non-believers, and of men and women, whether in front-line policing or in back-up administration, but national representativeness is vital for political stability.

The second part of our answer to the question is that there should not be too many police. Lightly policed peoples, like lightly governed peoples, are less likely to resist the authorities and are more likely to support their necessary activities. Lightly numbered police services are obliged to rely more on their interpersonal skills at street level than on their brute coercive powers; they have stronger incentives to stay within the rule of law, and to use their discretion carefully and sensitively, than do their counterparts in heavily numbered gendarmeries. Light-sizing is another reasonable benchmark for change, though we believe that, initially, it must be weighted less heavily than the need for representativeness.

Consider the RUC in the light of these two benchmarks. The most palpable fact is that nationalists and Catholics are extremely under-represented. While cultural Catholics make up around 43 per cent of Northern Ireland's population, they comprise merely 7.5 per cent of total RUC personnel (or 968 of 12,819 officers).[2] The current Catholic share is lower than at any time before 1969, even though the RUC has expanded threefold in size since then. Catholics are not only much less likely to be police officers than Protestants, they are also much less likely to join the police than minority groups in other democratic countries with histories of poor ethnic and communal relations. In 1983 blacks in the USA constituted 13.1 per cent of police officers, roughly their proportion of the population.[3] The Catholic proportion of RUC officers is, on the other hand, only

about one sixth of the Catholic share of Northern Ireland's population. We have no data on the political opinions of police officers but
suspect that voters for the SDLP are even less conspicuous than
Catholics, and that Sinn Féin voters are likely to be rather isolated
saboteurs.

There are, in short, reasonable doubts about whether the small
percentage of Catholic police officers can be considered, to para-
phrase Nye Bevan, 'authentic representatives' of the Catholic community. Catholics who join the RUC either are or must become
detached from the nationalist community. Alternatively, they are
recruited from that small minority of the Catholic population that
is not nationalist, or from Catholics who are not Northern Irish.
Academic sources, including one sympathetic to the RUC, have
noted that Catholic officers display attitudes that deviate from
mainstream views in the broader Catholic, let alone nationalist,
community and are in fact closer to Protestant and unionist attitudes.[4] Another academic has claimed that RUC figures on Catholics
are misleading as they appear to include those recruited from outside Northern Ireland, including from Britain.[5] The RUC insists, by
contrast, that it arrives at its figures by examining the Northern
Irish schools attended by its members, and that recruits from outside
Northern Ireland are not classified in the religious breakdown.[6] But
even if all Catholics in the RUC are Northern Irish Catholics, and
even if they are all secret admirers of Seamus Mallon, the composition of the force simply does not meet the benchmark for political
representativeness. Moreover, we must always remember that
Catholic and nationalist under-representation is not, of course, limited to the core police itself, but extends into the civilian Police
Authority which employs 3,500 workers. We are informed that
roughly 3,000, or 85 per cent, of these workers are Protestants.

The police service is also fundamentally unrepresentative of
Northern Ireland's population in its sexual ratios. Women outnum-
ber men in the population but constitute 12.6 per cent of the RUC
overall, and 10.8 per cent of RUC regulars (i.e., non-reservists).[7] The
under-representation of women in the police, while objectionable,
is not atypical when compared with other countries, and it is not a

critically important factor in heating local political divisions, which occur along national and cultural axes. But the sexual ratios of police personnel are relevant to resolving the main politically heated problem of representativeness. As nationalists and Catholics include a demographically predictable share of women (just over 50 per cent), any redress of the sexual imbalance, if handled correctly, would impact positively on the national and religious disparities. If the current police were to be restructured so that 50 per cent were men and 50 per cent were women, and if the new female recruits were drawn proportionately from cultural Catholics and cultural Protestants (43/57), the proportion of Catholics in the RUC would increase from 7.5 per cent to 23.6 per cent. Indeed, arguing that reforms are needed, at least partly, to correct the existing sexual imbalance has political advantages, as these would benefit Protestant as well as Catholic women, and would therefore be less divisive than the reforms that necessarily have to focus on the national and religious imbalance.

The second benchmark is also decisively failed by the contemporary RUC. It has too many members – especially if the paramilitary cease-fires become permanent and there is no return to large-scale violence. Civil libertarians and governmental cost-cutters alike correctly charge that Northern Ireland is over-policed, and have jointly called for 'downsizing'. As of November 1997, the RUC had 11,412 full-time officers as well as 1,407 part-timers. The current full-time complement is therefore over three times the number in place at the outset of the conflict,[8] and over three times the number of a comparable English or Scottish region (see Figure 3.1).

What is to be done?

As we have seen, there is no widespread agreement on how these problems of RUC unrepresentativeness and size should be resolved, or, indeed, on whether they are problems. Some have suggested that if there is a significant reduction in the scale of political violence the number of police officers will need to be reduced to around 4,000–4,500, while others accept a slightly higher range of

48

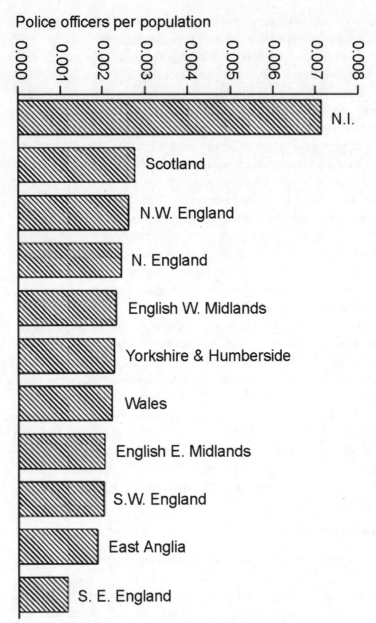

Figure 3.1 The comparative size of the RUC in the UK
Source: Regional Trends 1995 (London: HMSO)

4,600–5,700.[9] The RUC, and Her Majesty's Inspector of Constabulary, have argued that the service needs to retain somewhere between 6,000 and 8,000 officers.[10] Their reasoning is based on the plausible assumption that Northern Ireland will continue to have problems that similarly sized English counties do not have, but also upon the more questionable argument that, unlike its British counterparts, the RUC finds it difficult to get assistance from other police services in times of need.[11]

Size is connected with representativeness. The more police jobs there are, the easier it will be to increase the proportion of Catholic and nationalist officers without disadvantaging serving Protestant officers. Just as it was once considered necessary to allocate considerable resources to policing to stop violence, it may now be argued that considerable resources are needed to consolidate the peace process. We are willing to accept that argument in return for meaningful changes in the composition and nature of the police. On this basis we are prepared to accept the top figure suggested by the Chief Constable, 8,000 officers overall, at least for the next two decades.[12]

Downsizing the RUC by about one third, from 11,412 to 8,000 full-time officers (that is, a reduction of 3,412 positions), is a relatively easy task. Even if downsizing by attrition should be ruled out, because we respect the argument that the police need to regenerate themselves through continuing youthful recruitment, most of the cuts (2,939 of the 3,412 positions) could be achieved simply by eliminating the full-time RUC Reserve – whose members, unlike regulars, are on three-year contracts. This proposal might be considered too blunt because it would not, for instance, allow qualifications to be taken into account. If that argument is accepted, policy-makers could selectively eliminate positions in the Reserve while also refusing to allow police officers to continue beyond the age of compulsory retirement – in 1997, 372 were exempted from retirement at the normal age.[13] By itself, however, downsizing would not be likely to alter significantly the current religious and national imbalance. It is this particular personnel problem that generates the most controversy and needs greatest attention by the Patten Commission and the Secretary of State.

We recognise that not everyone accepts that a representative police service is a priority. One common view, especially held among unionists of goodwill, is that a representative police service is much less important than one that acts impartially. The Workers' Party, which takes this perspective, has argued that emphasising a 'representative' police service is harmful, because it involves an emphasis on group differences rather than on individualism,[14] which is not an argument one might expect from what is an allegedly Marxist and collectivist party. Those who share this position think that to allocate police positions on the basis of nationality, religion or ethnicity would entrench such differences when the public policy goal should be to eliminate them. This reasoning is either wilfully or wishfully unrealistic. Managing differences equally is often more effective and equitable than artificially eliminating them. A police service composed primarily of recruits from the dominant ethnic or national group will not be seen as impartial by members of excluded groups, irrespective of the behaviour of police officers. Such a service is also unlikely to be impartial in practice, as its officers are more likely to reflect the values of their own community of origin, and not those of others.

The key debate in policing reform should not therefore be over whether the police should be made more representative, but rather over how much more representative they should be. Significant numbers of unionists and nationalists believe there should be more Catholic officers. The major debate centres on the amount of change that is needed, and the period for achieving it. The position of the RUC and the Police Authority for Northern Ireland is that the application rate from the Catholic community should be increased so that it approaches the Catholic proportion of the population. In its 1997/8 report, the Police Authority signalled that it remained committed 'to the goal of attaining' a Catholic 'application rate of 35 per cent'.[15] To achieve more applications from Catholics, the RUC and the Police Authority cite the need for continuing ceasefires and political agreement, pointing out that the proportion of Catholic applications to the RUC nearly doubled from 11.7 per cent in 1993 to 20.3 per cent in 1995, after the IRA cease-fire of August

1994.[16] They also argue for the promotion of lawful affirmative action measures – such as gearing advertisements towards the minority – for equality of opportunity, and for the promotion of a neutral working environment.[17]

Achieving a 35 per cent Catholic application rate will not be easy. The rate for 1997, the latest year for which figures are available, and during which the IRA renewed its cease-fire (albeit in July), was only 14 per cent.[18] But let us accept, for the sake of argument, that through some means the Police Authority became successful in achieving its stated target of a 35 per cent Catholic application rate. This success, be it noted, would not necessarily translate into a 35 per cent Catholic *recruitment* rate. In fact, in most recent years Catholic applicants have been less likely to be hired than Protestants (see Table 3.1), contrary to the popular view that Catholic applicants to the RUC possess a 'green card' to a job in the police.[19] Moreover, given current hiring levels (roughly 200 vacancies per year), even a 35 per cent Catholic recruitment rate will not produce a police service that is 35 per cent Catholic until around the year 2026 (see Figure 3.2).[20] And, be it noted and underlined, even a 35 per cent Catholic police force would still mean that cultural Catholics, around 43 per cent of the population, were under-represented, and this under-representation is likely to become more obvious if, as seems likely, the cultural Catholic proportion of the population continues to grow.

Whatever Catholic numbers might be, it is extremely unlikely that nationalists are willing to wait for a generation before obtaining a nationally representative police service. If nationalists are to be accommodated, more radical policies than those envisaged by the Police Authority are necessary. These policies must have two tracks: one aimed at reducing the overall number of police officers, and the other at increasing the number of Catholics (and nationalist Catholics in particular). If it is agreed that the police service should have a total of 8,000 officers instead of the current 11,412, the government should aim to cut the number of currently serving officers to 5,000 over a medium-term period (say, around four years), while recruiting around 3,000 new officers. The government should then recruit

Table 3.1 (a)

Catholic applications, acceptances and wastage, full-time RUC, 1990–96

Year	Catholic applicants	Catholic acceptances	Catholic wastage*	Per cent of applicants who were Catholics	Per cent of acceptances who were Catholics	Per cent of wastage that was Catholic*
1990	116	15	14	10.4	11.4	6.9
1991	191	34	21	11.2	8.6	10.6
1992	231	26	10	10.0	8.0	6.3
1993	86	3	16	11.7	4.6	7.2
1994	954	26	19	15.9	13.9	11.2
1995	906	44	17	20.3	14.4	6.8
1996	768	N/a	N/a	15.9	N/a	N/a

Source: Northern Ireland Affairs Committee, *Composition, Recruitment and Training of the RUC*, Vol. II (London: Stationery Office, 1998), Appendix B, p. 14.
Notes: *Wastage is not defined by the RUC.   N/a = Not available. All percentage figures are rounded to one decimal place.

Table 3.1 (b)

Catholic applications, acceptances and wastage, full-time RUC Reserve, 1990–96

Year	Catholic applicants	Catholic acceptances	Catholic wastage*	Per cent of applicants who were Catholics	Per cent of acceptances who were Catholics	Per cent of wastage that was Catholic*
1990	67	10	8	9.0	10.0	8.0
1991	115	22	9	9.6	7.7	6.7
1992	175	23	10	9.3	8.2	5.6
1993	111	8	6	8.7	7.0	4.6
1994	–	–	–	–	–	–
1995	282	4	12	19.4	15.4	8.6
1996	255	N/a	N/a	17.8	N/a	N/a

Source: Northern Ireland Affairs Committee, *Composition, Recruitment and Training of the RUC*, Vol. II (London: Stationery Office, 1998), Appendix B, p. 14.
Notes: *Wastage is not defined by the RUC.   N/a = Not available. All percentage figures are rounded to one decimal place. 1994 entries for the RUC full-time Reserve are left blank and unexplained in the report.

53

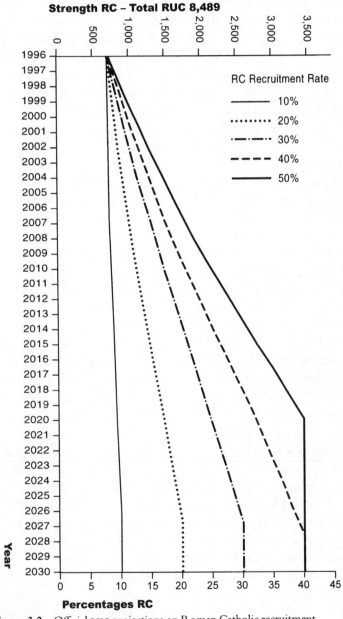

Figure 3.2 Official RUC projections on Roman Catholic recruitment

Source: As in Table 3.1, p. 16.

Catholics disproportionately during this transition period. A 93 per cent Catholic hiring rate during the transition would produce a police service that is 40 per cent Catholic, and roughly representative of Northern Ireland's population.[21] This twin-track strategy could and should be managed in such a way that it increases the representation of other under-represented groups, such as loyalists from working-class backgrounds, and, of course, women.[22]

A large and reasonably quick induction of Catholic officers along the lines suggested here would increase Catholic confidence in the police tremendously. It would also make it easier for many Catholics to contemplate joining the police, as their behaviour would be in line with significant numbers of their community in their age range. And finally, such a rapid induction is essential to the changing of the internal culture of the police. Small inductions of Catholics, particularly over a protracted period, would run the risk that such recruits would take on the force's existing culture, as has happened until now in Northern Ireland, and has happened in US or British police services, when small numbers of blacks were introduced into largely white police services.[23]

Such a transition would create opposition within the unionist community. However, the UK government would be in a position to explain, correctly, that police numbers are being maintained at higher levels than strictly necessary in order to facilitate representativeness, and that the alternative to this strategy is a smaller police service – in which similar numbers of Protestant positions would be lost anyway.[24] Unionist opposition may also be minimised if the UK government acts generously towards police retirees, and if it is made clear that the new appointments are not merely necessary for winning nationalist support for the new police, but also wholly justified, as we shall maintain, on efficiency and merit grounds.

An important task for the UK government in managing the transition to a representative police force will be to minimise the impact on those officers who are released. The government's first step should be to stop renewing the three-year contracts of members of the RUC Reserve. Most of the Reserve should be released over a three-year period, while particularly deserving members should be allowed to transfer into the regular police service. Generous severance packages linked to years of service should be paid. The elimination of the Reserve, assuming 400 transfers to the regular police, would achieve around 2,500 of the needed cuts. During the four-year transition period, around 800 police officers could be expected to retire.[25] This would mean that a further 3,100 officers would have to be released if the number of currently serving officers was to be reduced to 5,000. This further downsizing should be achieved, in the first instance, by generous and voluntary early-retirement packages. Such packages formed an essential part of transitional policing arrangements in South Africa,[26] and the UK government has already indicated that it will approach downsizing with 'sensitivity and generosity'.[27] Nor should the government's incentive package be limited to cash payments: it must examine ways of retraining police officers for productive jobs in other sectors of the economy.

Providing the UK government is generous, these incentives should be enough to achieve the necessary reductions. If they are not, the balance will have to be achieved through redundancies. These would have to be designed to avoid the normal crude 'last in, first out' practice.[28] Officers who have disciplinary records, or who have not responded well to the police's training programme in community awareness, should be considered more eligible for redundancies than others. Officers made redundant should be eligible for any job-retraining programmes. Some of them, though probably not a large number, could be offered positions in other police services in the UK that have vacancies.[29] It might also be possible for some officers to move from full-time to part-time status, as is already possible under 1996 legislation.

It is difficult to be precise about the costs involved in downsizing the police along the lines we are suggesting here. The early-retirement and severance packages that are offered to each individual would vary depending on service and rank. However, if we assume that an average of £50,000 per individual was required, and that 5,600 payments would be made (6,400 cuts minus 800 normal retirements), the total cost to the Exchequer would be £280 million, presumably phased. While this is a considerable sum, it represents less than two thirds (64 per cent) of the full-time RUC's annual salary bill of £439 million.[30] As the annual total police salary bill would be reduced by roughly 30 per cent as a result of downsizing from 11,412 officers to 8,000, the cost of the early retirement/ redundancy packages would be recouped in just over two years from savings on salary. In any case, since some such transition is necessary for peace, and as peace will have some advantages for the Exchequer, it would be wrong to focus on the short-term economic costs.

The second track towards achieving a representative police service involves finding ways to hire Catholics and other underrepresented groups disproportionately. One way to achieve this involves positive discrimination, in this case giving *qualified* Catholics the edge over *qualified* Protestants, in order to achieve specific quotas. There are a variety of precedents for this in other liberal democracies, for example, in Canada and South Africa. Governments in these countries have deliberately positively discriminated in favour of under-represented groups as an act of public policy, particularly in the police service where it is considered especially important to have broad representation. The UUP committee set up in 1922 to organise the RUC recognised the value of proportionality over strict implementation of the merit principle, when it recommended that one third of the new force should be Catholic.[31]

The promotion of proportionality or quotas in policing over strict definitions of merit might be justified because it is necessary to:

- create a representative and broadly accepted police force,
- increase nationalist support for the political status quo, and
- reduce the significant employment gap between Catholics and Protestants.[32]

It could also be argued that any deviation from individual equality of opportunity to equality of result would be temporary in nature, and would have to last only so long as is necessary to correct the current imbalance in police personnel. After that, the police would have to rely on difference-blind hiring policies. We believe that if no other way can be found to create a representative police service, positive discrimination is something the UK government will have to consider.

Positive discrimination, however, is illegal under the Fair Employment Act (1989). While this act, like any other, could be amended by parliament, the current government remains committed to recruitment on grounds of merit.[33] There is also strong general support for the merit principle in both communities. Unionists of all stripes would be likely to protest strongly at positive discrimination, and Catholic or nationalist recruits who were hired because of positive discrimination, and even those who were not, might well feel stigmatised. Even the Labour MP Ken Livingstone, a stout defender of northern nationalists, has argued that positive discrimination in the police would be 'totally counter-productive' and that 'people have to be advanced on merit'.[34]

In this context the UK government will no doubt, at least in the first instance, seek to ensure that all new hiring is done in conformity with the merit principle. This need not mean accepting, however, the narrow description of merit that forms the basis of current hiring practices. The Patten Commission and the UK government should argue instead that as effective policing requires strong links between the police and the people they serve, and as it is impossible to create these if the police are overwhelmingly from one community, so more Catholics, especially nationalist Catholics, are needed on efficiency grounds. Part of the reason why more unionists than nationalists trust the RUC, and why more intelligence is forthcoming from loyalist than from republican areas, is that the RUC is overwhelmingly Protestant.[35] The RUC's first Inspector-General recognised this in the early 1920s: 'It is quite useless to expect to obtain any information from the RC areas unless there are RC police and detectives. The efficiency of the force suffers at present from a lack of RC police.'[36] Membership of, and familiarity with the norms and culture of, the nationalist community should be considered a criterion of merit in any rational public administration in Northern Ireland, something to be taken into consideration along with other criteria during the hiring process.[37] If nationalists can be encouraged to apply to be police officers, and if there is recognition that they possess a resource the police currently lack and need, then the disproportionate hiring of nationalists is required on meritorious grounds for the tasks in hand (unless one assumes that nationalists are less intelligent or, on average, substantially less educated than unionists in ways that would impair their performance as police officers).

Another way to achieve the same result, while still conforming with merit criteria, would be for the UK government to insist that new recruits should come from or reside in the locality that they police, and that all regions of Northern Ireland should be fairly represented in the police service. In this case, the policing authorities would justify their decisions on the grounds that it is essential for a police officer to be familiar with the territory being policed, and that if 'community policing' is to take root, it should be conducted by officers either indigenous to or now living in (or even willing to live in) the relevant districts. As most nationalist (and most loyalist) communities are currently policed by officers who live far outside the policing area,[38] the effect of such a new recruitment policy would be to create openings for those living or prepared to live in such areas. The 'core skills' identified by the RUC as required in a police officer do not at present include knowledge either of the nationalist or unionist community or of many localities in Northern Ireland – something that can rapidly be remedied.

A third way to increase the proportion of nationalists, without resorting to discrimination on the basis of religious social origins, is to require the police to consider specific educational qualifications, including courses and diplomas in policing, during hiring. Pre-recruitment educational programmes could then be targeted at areas of social need, which are disproportionately nationalist. If government grants for undertaking such programmes were limited to those who were unemployed, for example, Catholic males should benefit at twice the rate of Protestant males, given that these are their comparative positions in the labour market. While the privileging of Catholics as Catholics is illegal under the Fair Employment Act, it is permissible to target areas and classes.[39]

Some of these policies can and should be used to ensure better loyalist representation in the police. While the police are mostly from unionist backgrounds, and some come from working-class loyalist districts, few officers live in loyalist areas. As the Progressive Unionist Party has pointed out, policemen recruited from and living in loyalist areas would be more likely to know who the criminals are: 'It is accepted that policemen could hardly live safely in working-class Catholic areas, but the fact is that nowadays policemen rarely live within any working-class precincts ... Gone is the "local Bobby" known to all his neighbours, and ... likely to be aware of who the local troublemakers are.'[40]

So far, we have discussed the religious and national imbalance in the RUC at an aggregate level, and have avoided commenting on differential imbalances within the policing hierarchy. Catholics are slightly better represented in senior ranks than at the rank of constable, comprising 10 per cent of inspectors and chief inspectors (64 of 643), 17 per cent of superintendents and chief superintendents (27 of 160), and 11 per cent of assistant chief constables (1 of 9).[41] However, Catholics remain strikingly under-represented in even these ranks when compared to their share of the population, male or female, or the population of working age.[42] Even if more Catholics are recruited into the police service at junior levels, there will continue to be a serious imbalance at senior levels. One way for the UK government to address this difficulty rapidly would be to consider lateral transfers from other executive-level positions into the senior ranks of the police. Some senior jobs – for example, in the community relations, forensics or personnel departments – do not require a specific background in the police, and could be filled effectively by those with suitable credentials earned elsewhere. The government could also consider the secondment of senior officers from the Garda Síochána, and it could seek proactively to recruit senior Garda Síochána officers to permanent jobs, until there are enough senior officers from nationalist communities in Northern Ireland.

Eligibility of offenders under scheduled offences

One thorny question about recruitment is whether ex-paramilitaries should be eligible for police membership. Precedents for recruiting ex-paramilitaries formerly opposed to the state, or formerly engaged in civil wars, into the police and armed services exist in a range of countries, including South Africa and El Salvador. After the partition of Ireland, the RUC and the Garda Síochána received significant influxes from the UVF and IRA respectively. In the case of the Garda Síochána, the experiment eventually involved the successful integration of some former members of groups that had been engaged in a bitter civil war. Recruiting ex-paramilitaries into the police provides them with jobs and gives them a material stake in the new political arrangements. There are also clear advantages to operating a general policy of inclusiveness when trying to reach a durable peace after decades of conflict.[43]

Nevertheless, certain abuses of human rights should render individuals (whether ex-paramilitary, or ex-military, or ex-police) ineligible for membership in a police service. Extending eligibility to people irrespective of their past actions would strain the credibility of the new police, and would be seized on by those who are opposed to change, and who want to prevent the acceptance of the reforms advocated here. Our position, and that of several other commentators, is that former membership in a paramilitary organisation should not itself render an individual ineligible for police membership, although the commission of serious crimes, especially crimes against persons, should.[44] There should be no double standard here: police officers convicted of human rights abuses or scheduled offences against persons should also not be eligible to be re-recruited into the police or the armed services.

Allowing *former* paramilitaries to join the police is not the same as handing over the policing of certain areas to paramilitary organisations, as opponents of the proposal fear – and scaremongers suggest – will happen. Police membership must be incompatible with paramilitary membership, whether of organisations that have cease-fires or not. Nor would the presence of former paramilitaries mean that the police should be allowed to administer punishments without due legal process. All police, including those operating in republican and loyalist strongholds, would have to be under the control of, and accountable to, duly constituted political and legal authorities.

Conclusion

Constructing a representative police should bring a number of benefits. It will increase nationalist confidence that the police service(s) represent(s) everybody. It will erode the partisan unionist culture in the current police force in a more effective way than can ever be done by the RUC's provision of 'cultural awareness' training for Protestant officers. By making available a number of high-paying jobs for nationalists, it will also go some way towards meeting the government's goal of eroding the unemployment gap, and the comparative income gap, between Protestants and Catholics. By enhancing nationalist support for legitimate policing, and for the new political status quo, such change will also benefit the unionist community. As the leaders of the UUP have realised, the long-term future of the Union will be better secured if it can be demonstrated to nationalists that it works in a manner that is fair and just. Unionists should also appreciate that a representative police force will be a more effective police force, as it will have more effective communication with the nationalist community than the RUC has ever enjoyed. Loyalists, as well as nationalists and republicans, could be expected to gain from some of the changes recommended here. That is not to say that change will be painless or costless. There will be some long-term economic costs for the unionist community from downsizing police numbers, but many of these costs are an unavoidable consequence of the transition to peace. In the short term, these costs will be offset considerably if the government is generous in providing compensation and retraining.

The creation of police job openings for Catholics, however, will not be enough to produce a dramatic increase in Catholic applications. Northern Catholics are not like racial minorities in the United States and elsewhere who are (or have been) under-represented because of discriminatory hiring practices. Catholics are also under-represented in the RUC because they consider it a nationally unacceptable police force, and do not apply to join it. Creating a representative police service therefore requires changes that make the police more acceptable to nationalists as well as policies that ease the hiring of Catholics. Such changes must be directed towards creating a nationally impartial policing service and towards enhancing local and democratic control over policing by the communities being policed. These objectives are discussed in the next three chapters.

4

Towards a nationally impartial police

RUC needs new name and uniform, Alliance [Party] tells Patten
BELFAST TELEGRAPH, 18 OCTOBER 1998

It is our premise that the police have to be representative in their origins if they are to be accepted throughout Northern Ireland. If they are not, no numbers of courts, jails or police will enable the law to work as intended. But making the police representative will be no easy task, even if the political will now exists to ensure that they are. Nationalists are unlikely to be willing to join any policing service(s) in large numbers, despite the attractions of relatively high pay, unless there are other major reforms beyond those aimed at transforming the backgrounds of recruits. Nationalists who would join under current arrangements are seen as pariahs by many of their co-nationalists, and as deeply suspect – just like those Catholics already in the RUC. Republicans, nearly one fifth of the Northern Irish electorate, regard Catholics who joined the RUC as like the blacks who joined the South African police under the apartheid regime, collaborators with an unjust regime. The problem is that most Catholics, most northern nationalists, and all republicans, regard the RUC as a unionist police force, a partisan force.

The RUC has a unionist title, and unionist icons, a fact recognised by the Alliance Party, the party that has the best claim to represent 'others', that is those who do not customarily identify with Northern Ireland's dominant political identities. The RUC has been, and still is, imbued with a unionist political ethos. It has defended the Union against nationalists in a martial manner. Its officers have patrolled predominantly nationalist districts in the company of the B Specials, the UDR, and the British Army. They have implemented internment without trial, maltreated people suspected of being paramilitaries, organised supergrasses, fired plastic bullets at unarmed civilians and shot-to-kill. The image of the RUC among Catholics and nationalists is worse than that of the mere 'peeler'. It is so negative that one moderate observer, who is pessimistic about the prospects for police reform, has argued that 'the association of policeman and Catholic [is] antithetical in . . . identity'.[1]

Self-styled 'realists' conclude that Northern Ireland's police, whether they be the RUC or some other service(s), can never be completely impartial between nationalists and unionists, especially as long as Northern Ireland is part of the Union, and certainly as long as the police are responsible for protecting and enforcing British law. These 'realists' include both hardline unionists and some IRA veterans. In both cases the conclusion is a premature and self-interested counsel – of hope and despair. In fact, much can be done to remove national partisanship in policing. One consequence of the full implementation of the Good Friday Agreement is that the new constitutional arrangements, and laws passed under them, in principle enjoy the formal consent of most nationalists and a majority of the Northern Irish electorate. New policing arrangements that are consistent with the Agreement can, in principle, operate with bi-national consent. How so?

The Royal Ulster Constabulary and symbolic change

The names, symbols and icons attached to the RUC are, for the most part, solidly unionist. The force's name is the Royal Ulster Constabulary, a name devised by the UUP, and one that reflects an obvious unionist bias, a bias inherited from its predecessor, the Royal Irish Constabulary. The RUC has only three problems with its name. One: it is 'Royal', demonstrating a unionist, monarchist and anti-republican political identity. Two: its territorial reference is to 'Ulster', which either emphasises its unionist identity in bold, because 'Ulster' is unionists' partisan term for Northern Ireland,[2] or it is a geographical and legal error, because Ulster includes three counties in the Republic of Ireland over which the RUC has no jurisdiction. Three: it is a 'Constabulary', which is antiquated in its connotations, and which has coercive suggestions of a gendarmerie unsuitable for a rights-defending, democratic and modern police service. This name is not carved in stone, nor would a change to it necessarily have to take place at the expense of the interests or identity of the unionist community.[3]

The name of the police has in fact already been very slightly modified in the Police Act of 1998. The RUC is now a component part of the Northern Ireland Police Service – this umbrella organisation incorporates the RUC as well as traffic wardens and the civilian employees of the Police Authority for Northern Ireland. Perhaps this is the first step in an incremental process of rebaptism, a rebaptism in impartiality. We hope so, and see no good reason why this should not happen.

It must be emphasised that the RUC is not merely royalist by name. Until recent legislation was passed by the Westminster parliament, RUC recruits were obliged to swear an oath of allegiance to the Queen. Staff and officers of the RUC display pictures of the Queen in police stations, including in their Community Relations department. The Union Jack is hoisted above RUC stations on public holidays, including, until recently, on the Twelfth of July – Orangeman's Day. This is the day on which large numbers of Protestants celebrate the historic victory of King William of Orange over the forces of James II in 1690, and one on which large numbers of them wave Union Jacks to celebrate their political identity, and when some of them strive to do so in the immediate environs of the homes of northern nationalists.[4] Even the RUC's crown-and-harp emblem, worn on officers' caps, which some believe appropriate in the light of Northern Ireland's historical divisions, is disliked by some nationalists – because the crown is above the harp, perhaps suggesting Ireland's subjugation by Britain.[5] Whatever the psychological and historical merits of these arguments they are deeply held, and, in any case, the claim to national impartiality in icons is exposed when one realises that the shoulder epaulettes of RUC officers display crowns rather than harps and crowns – a sign that might suggest that the arms of the police are more royalist than their heads.

Supporters of the RUC's existing symbolism employ two mental defences, which are mutually inconsistent. One strategy is to argue that to quarrel on symbolic matters is essentially trivial. Most serious people, so it is implied, do not and should not take such matters to be important. In 1996 the former Northern Ireland Security Minister, Conservative MP Sir John Wheeler, stated that people were more interested in 'quality of service' than in 'symbols'.[6] Impartial listeners to such arguments are immediately tempted to respond by asking, 'If these matters are trivial then why is so much time and energy devoted to opposing trivial changes?' The Chief Constable, Ronnie Flanagan, giving evidence to the Northern Ireland Affairs Committee, maintained that the issue of the RUC's name 'was not a major factor' in the debate over the police, and that changing its name would not help him recruit Catholics.[7] The RUC even maintains that the display of the Queen's portrait and the waving of the Union flag above its stations are consistent with a 'neutral working environment'[8] – a preposterous argument that is perhaps less surprising when one recalls that public and private sector employers are required to maintain a neutral working environment under existing fair employment legislation.

The other tack of supporters of the existing name, symbols and regalia of the RUC is very different, and very inconsistent with the first. This strategy suggests that symbols are very important, so important that to focus on these divisive features of identity politics is to preclude more accommodating or reformist possibilities. Here the proposition is not that to propose such changes is to engage in trivial politics; far from it: it is instead claimed that such changes must have a deeply divisive zero-sum character – one side must necessarily lose exactly whatever the other would gain. In its 1996 White Paper on policing, the Conservative government argued against interfering with the name, symbols and iconography of the RUC because there was 'no consensus' on the subject. This suggested that any changes would be zero-sum, and that while some (nationalists) sought change, most (unionists) did not. Robert McCartney MP was more forthright during the parliamentary debate on the Police Bill in December 1997: the symbols are unionists', and unionists embrace them because their identity is under threat from an Irish nationalist onslaught.[9] The present position of the Police Authority is that the name and the harp and crown symbols should remain unchanged, but that the Chief Constable and Secretary of State should 'review' the number of days on which the Union flag is flown.[10]

Before evaluating the merits of these mutually inconsistent defences let us examine some facts about how the RUC's name, emblems and symbols are seen by nationalists and unionists. There is considerable evidence from political parties' statements, from commission reports and from opinion surveys that nationalists object to them. Contrary to the Chief Constable's view, the Opsahl Commission reported that the 'failure' of a 'Crown' police to shake off the symbols of the unionist state appeared time and time again as an explanation of Catholics' reluctance to join the RUC.[11] The results of an independent survey conducted in December 1997 found that 77 per cent of Catholics thought it was either 'essential' (59 per cent) or 'desirable' (18 per cent) that the RUC be given a new name, and a mere 3–4 per cent of Catholics found this idea 'unacceptable'. Moreover, 76 per cent of Catholics thought it either 'essential' (58 per cent) or 'desirable' (18 per cent) that the police be given new emblems and symbols, while only 4 per cent found this to be unacceptable.[12] Protestants, however, registered strong opposition to both changes, with around 60 per cent finding changes to the name and symbols to be 'unacceptable'.[13] In its latest report, the Police Authority acknowledges the existence of deep divisions on the RUC's symbols.[14] This brief résumé of the evidence suggests that

Sir John Wheeler's strategy does not connect with reality: the name, symbols and regalia attached to the RUC are deeply important and views about them are deeply held. But need this mean that any change would have to be zero-sum in nature? An affirmative answer would be too hasty.

What position ought the Patten Commission to take? Its terms of reference mean that it should not do what the Conservative government did in 1996, and argue that a lack of consensus for change means that the status quo must be retained. Such a response would merely give a veto to the historically dominant side, and thereby maintain an unjust situation. Nothing in its terms of reference requires the Commission to keep the name of the RUC: a reading of these terms of reference makes it plain that the RUC is only referred to in the past or present tense, and not in the future tense (see Appendix A to this book). Nothing subsequently said by a UK prime minister or ministers after the signing of the British–Irish Agreement in April 1998 alters the Patten Commission's terms of reference, which are solemn components of an interparty and intergovernmental agreement.

What the Patten Commission should do, and indeed is obliged to do, is as follows. It should either ensure that the police's name, symbols and mandate are fully neutral and impartial, or that they are fully bi-national and impartial. There are, in short, two routes to impartiality. Neither requires the Patten Commission to revise the names and symbols of the RUC in an overtly pro-nationalist direction, for example by renaming the force with an exclusively Gaelic title, such as Córas Síochána Thuaisceart Éireann (which would roughly translate as the 'Peacekeeping Authority of Northern Ireland'). The Patten Commission is not obliged to make a symbolic recommendation that would be zero-sum in character, either unionist or nationalist. As in many policies there are several third ways.

An impartial and neutral English-language naming strategy would mean that the main body of police officers in Northern Ireland could be called the Northern Ireland Police Service. This title has many advantages. It accurately describes the area over which the police have jurisdiction; it is already the name of the umbrella organisation of which the RUC is a part; Northern Ireland is now an entity officially recognised by nationalists, unionists and others in a constitutional referendum; the title appears modern; and the proposed title is relatively non-coercive. It is a name that both unionists and nationalists who endorsed the Good Friday Agreement can support with full ideological consistency. Hardline unionists who are unpersuaded by this argument might think of our proposed change as 'integrationist', and properly British in character. In Great Britain the vast majority of policing units are not 'Royal'; they make no inaccurate geographical descriptions of their powers that imply jurisdiction in other sovereign states of the European Union; and they prefer to be called 'services' rather than constabularies. Hardline republicans, by contrast, might think of our proposed change as 'transitional', and properly Irish in character. As long as Northern Ireland remains part of the Union with the consent of the people of Ireland it must have policing arrangements that recognise its existence.

An alternative route to impartiality involves bi-national and bi-lingual naming. The new central police service could have two names, one in English and one in Gaelic: for example, the RUC and Constáblacht Ríoga Uladh, or the Northern Ireland Police Service and Seirbhís Phóilíos Thuaisceart Éireann (a very literal and stilted translation) or Córas Síochána Thuaisceart Éireann (a more idiomatic translation).[15] The first double naming would have the advantage of satisfying both national languages but at the cost of failing to have a name with which nationalists can politically identify. For that reason we expect this proposal to be less widely acceptable, not least to the 'others' – Northern Ireland's often-forgotten minority. The second proposal we think has a fair chance of eventually achieving a widespread consensus, in either of its Gaelic variants. Our preference, having taken idiomatic guidance from the Dublin Institute for Advanced Studies, is for the Gaelic title of the Northern Ireland Police Service to be Córas Síochána Thuaisceart Éireann.

If, as we will later argue, there should be more than one police

service, the same impartial reasoning we have invoked should be
applied case by case by the Patten Commission and future law-
makers: either there should be no unionist or nationalist symbols
attached to the police service(s), or both forms of symbolism should
be allowed simultaneously, while recalling the interests and identity
of the others who are neither unionist nor nationalist.[16] For example, to help remove doubts about the police's impartiality between
nationalists and unionists, a new police charter should include a sen-
tence that would read along the following lines:

> The police service welcomes within its ranks all law-abiding citi-
> zens, including those who support the maintenance of the Union
> and those who aspire to a united Ireland, as well as those who have
> other political opinions about the past, present and future of
> Northern Ireland.

Any such charter should make it clear that one of the police's fundamental values is impartiality between the unionist and nationalist
communities, and others, and not simply impartiality among individuals. This change would merely put in writing what several senior RUC officers claim is already the case in practice – so it should
therefore be easy to implement. Measures along these lines would
create a genuinely neutral working environment for Northern Ireland's diverse peoples, fully in keeping with the letter and spirit of
fair employment legislation.[17]

It is probably true, as the Chief Constable argues, that changes to
the name of the RUC and the symbolic dimensions of its uniforms
and working environs would, on their own, have limited effects on
nationalists' overall assessments of the police service. However, this
is not, as he seems to think, an effective argument for avoiding
changes to its name and symbols. It is, on the contrary, an argument
that suggests that changes should not be limited to symbols. Robert
McCartney's view that unionists want to retain these symbols because they are faced with a nationalist onslaught, made some sense
before the republican cease-fires and before the Good Friday Agreement. It makes much less sense today. The Agreement, endorsed by
London and Dublin, accepted by all significant Irish nationalist
parties, including Sinn Féin, and solidly ratified by nationalists in

referendums in both parts of Ireland, specifies that a united Ireland cannot be achieved unless there is majority consent for it in Northern Ireland, and it specifies changes to articles 2 and 3 of the Republic's Constitution that are conditional upon the implementation of the Agreement. In this new context, unionists have much less reason to fear that their constitutional future is under threat, or that they are facing an escalating nationalist assault. More far-sighted unionists than Robert McCartney know that neutral or bi-national symbols, which everyone could embrace, have a better chance of solidifying the Union through reconciling nationalists to its existence than does a Union that symbolically remains a unionist Union.

Culture and training

The RUC is nationally imbalanced not only in personnel and symbols, but also, unsurprisingly, in its internal culture. Brewer and Magee's study found that it was overwhelmingly Protestant in its ethos. Officers read Protestant newspapers, supported Protestant soccer teams, and shared the general outlook of the Protestant community, including presumably its political views.[18] Some Catholic officers, in order to fit in, expressed exaggerated anti-Catholic bigotry. A survey of part-time members of the RUC found that the Protestant organisational culture led to Catholic officers having to detach themselves from the Catholic community.[19] Other research observes that the locker-room banter or 'canteen culture' in the RUC is profoundly anti-Catholic.[20] This view is held by an ex-member of the Police Authority and a former reporter of the police's activities.[21] The RUC's own research unit, M5, reported in a leaked confidential report in December 1997 that sectarian harassment of Catholic officers by their colleagues is rife: 63 per cent of the Catholic officers who responded, by contrast with 10 per cent of Protestants, claimed they had been harassed.[22] These findings are hardly surprising: when a police force is overwhelmingly recruited from one national community in a deeply divided territory, it would be unrealistic to expect its officers not to share the strong sentiments, values, attitudes, beliefs and prejudices of their co-nationals. The dominance of the Protestant and unionist culture in the RUC helps to explain not only why nationalists do not join the police,[23] but why the wider nationalist community does not identify with it.

The RUC has tried to resolve the problem of its internal cultural imbalance through the development of training programmes in cultural awareness. An internal RUC working party established to address the question of Catholic under-representation concluded in February 1998 that 'much more must be done to eliminate both perceived and actual harassment'.[24] One obvious problem is the small amount of time devoted to community awareness training. Currently, only 8 per cent of the initial training programme of twenty-five weeks is spent on community awareness training,[25] arguably one of the most serious difficulties the RUC faces. Another problem is that the programmes are taught almost exclusively by RUC officers, and take place within the RUC Training Centre, which led the working party to conclude they were 'very introspective'.[26]

One way to respond to introspection would be to end it. The UK government should remove control over training, including community awareness training, from the police and give it to a civilian Police Training Agency. The director of this new agency would be an independent public official, and would operate in consultation with a board which would have representation from the police as well as human rights agencies, including statutory bodies such as the new Human Rights Commission and the new Police Complaints Ombudsman, and non-governmental organisations such as the Committee for the Administration of Justice and Amnesty International. The agency would, for the time being, operate under the authority of the UK government but could report to the British–Irish Intergovernmental Conference until such time as control over policing is devolved to the Northern Ireland government. The agency would be charged with finding the best expertise available, within the RUC or its successor(s), other police forces, and civil society. To facilitate nationality awareness, a component of the training should take place in the Republic of Ireland and in Great Britain. Applicants to the police could be given training credit for related skills and courses gained before applying to join the police.

Training programmes for new recruits, however good, will not resolve the problems identified by the RUC's own internal research. Training will have to apply to all ranks and to all currently serving officers. It should also be continuous, taking place not only during the first six months of the policing career, but at regular intervals thereafter. There should be regular exchanges with police services outside Northern Ireland, including those in Great Britain and the Republic of Ireland. But even if training is revised along these lines, it cannot serve as a substitute for having Catholics and especially nationalists in the police service. As Jones and Newburn observe, 'culture is usually too resilient to be affected by training'.[27] Their reasoning underlines the necessity both of changing the composition of the police, as recommended in Chapter 3, and of the other changes discussed in this and subsequent chapters.

Police membership in secret or partisan organisations

It is currently possible for RUC officers to be members of secret and sectarian organisations, including the Loyal Orders (Orange Order, Royal Black Preceptory and Apprentice Boys) and Freemasons. One of these, the Orange Order, tells each of its members to 'strenuously oppose the fatal errors and doctrines of the Church of Rome and scrupulously avoid countenancing (by his presence or otherwise) any act or ceremony of Popish worship'. It is also vigorously committed to preserving the Union between Great Britain and Northern Ireland; its original oath went as follows: 'I . . . do solemnly swear that I will, to the utmost of my power, support and defend the King and his heirs as long as he or they support the Protestant ascendancy.'[28]

The Chief Constable of the RUC appears to believe that only a small minority of RUC officers are in the Orange Order, but one academic researcher has estimated that as many as 2,000 police officers are Orangemen.[29] According to the Chief Constable, in his evidence to the Northern Ireland Affairs Committee in November 1997, the Loyal Orders' members in the RUC do not have a 'significant' effect on Catholic recruitment: 'Certainly in all the evidence in surveys, there is no evidence that this [police membership in Loyal Orders] is significant.'[30] One problem with this response, however, is that the Police Authority's surveys do not list police membership of Loyal Orders as one of the reasons respondents might pick to explain why Catholics do not join the RUC (see Table 1.1, page 10). An independent survey conducted in the month after the committee hearings showed that 69 per cent of Catholics thought it was 'essential' that police officers should not be allowed to be members of Loyal Orders, while another 12 per cent thought this would be 'desirable'.[31] Those who do not share the Chief Constable's insights into non-existent survey data are more likely to be persuaded that the presence of members of the Loyal Orders in the RUC's ranks reinforces its image as a unionist and Protestant force and calls into question its ability impartially to police Loyal Order marches. The Orange presence also helps many Catholics to accept Sinn Féin's argument that the RUC and the largest Loyal Order are inextricably linked.

The Chair of the Police Federation, the police's functional equivalent of a trade union,[32] and leaders of the Orange Order see nothing wrong with such overlapping membership. Others, including the Chief Constable,[33] Her Majesty's Inspector of Constabulary,[34] and the Police Authority,[35] have acknowledged that dual membership creates an impression that the police might not be objective – though, surprisingly, they do not accept that Orange Order membership might render the RUC or an individual officer partial in practice. The Hunt Committee raised the problem of police membership of the Orange Order as early as 1969, but failed to make a recommendation on the question. Both the Police Authority and the Chief Constable have a solution: to call for membership to be registered with the RUC's hierarchy, but not with the public, for security reasons.[36] The reasoning is that such a registry would create greater incentives for Orange police officers to be impartial than is currently the case, and that it would help to alleviate Catholic concerns about police bias. The reluctance to ban Orange membership is based on the proposition that a ban would curtail important civil liberties of officers.

It is difficult to take these arguments seriously, but we owe them the respect of a formal rebuttal. The idea of a registry is not completely without merit, but it seems clear that Catholic confidence in the police's impartiality would be heightened much further if Orange Order and other secret order membership were banned among police officers. Victorian liberals had no difficulty in banning the police from membership in such organisations. They prohibited such overlapping membership in the Royal Irish Constabulary. No human right is at stake here. To be a police officer and a member of a secret or sectarian organisation simultaneously is not a right or liberty respected in the Bill of Rights of any liberal democracy that we know of. Indeed, in many liberal democracies, civil servants in particular strategic positions (such as ambulance workers, or electoral returning officers) are denied permission to engage in what many would regard as more legitimate political activities that are permitted to others. They are often stopped from striking, standing for election, joining a political party, or even voting, if such steps further the public good of procedural fairness in political institutions.

If an outright ban on membership of such organisations is deemed unacceptable, for reasons that we cannot personally understand, there is a fallback position: to ban membership for new recruits to the RUC, as the Northern Ireland Affairs Committee has recently recommended in its July 1998 report.[37] The fallback argument rests on the claim that it is more invasive of liberty to change the rules in midstream for serving officers than it is to establish new rules for prospective applicants; and that the fallback proposal has political advantages, as it will help to minimise resentment and opposition to reform among serving officers, and will therefore appeal to more unionists of goodwill than an outright ban. Perhaps. The compromise fallback would have some chance of being accepted provided it is carried out in conformity with all the other changes recommended in this book, particularly the composition changes suggested in Chapter 3.

Impartiality must apply universally. The Patten Commission

must suggest bans that are implemented in an even-handed way. Bans must apply equally to Catholic sectarian organisations, such as the Ancient Order of Hibernians (AOH), as well as to the Loyal Orders and Freemasons, though we are not aware that there are officers who belong to the AOH. Contrary to the view of the RUC and the Police Authority, such a ban would not merely increase the 'impression' that the police are impartial. By making it impossible for those committed to sectarian organisations to become police officers, it would make it more likely that the police would be non-sectarian in attitudes and practice. We would go one step further and ban police officers from belonging to political parties, not on the grounds that political parties are either secretive or sectarian in Northern Ireland, but because a representative but impartial police service requires this form of depoliticisation.

Normalisation – take two

As we argued in Chapter 2, much of the current dissatisfaction with policing in nationalist and, more recently, in loyalist districts stems from the counterinsurgency role of the RUC – it is heavily armed, and heavily legally equipped with emergency powers. Despite the attempt by Lord Hunt to create a normal police in the early 1970s, the government, in response to the security threat, continued to use the police in a paramilitary role. The RUC was rearmed after only a very short period of being disarmed. Normalisation 1970s-style did not mean the establishment of a normal police force: on the contrary, it was a strategic attempt by the British government to create the impression of normality abroad, by hiding the army's salience in the maintenance of order, and by giving the police the vanguard role in maintaining security against (mostly) nationalist insurgents.

The state's response was wrong and counterproductive, but it was understandable, if not forgivable, given the violent campaign launched against it by republicans. Things are different now. With luck and good politics the war is over. The commitment of the major paramilitary groups to political dialogue, the achievement of the Good Friday Agreement, the passage of the referendums in both parts of Ireland – all suggest a meaningful normalisation of policing can occur. Civil policing of the type envisaged by Hunt and others is now feasible.

The first step is to ensure that the police service or services are no longer routinely armed. The parties to the Good Friday Agreement have already accepted that disarmament should happen, providing there is a peaceful environment. Police stations should be converted from the current forbidding military-style fortresses to a larger number of more accessible stations, located close to the areas being policed. In addition to multifunction stations, there should be smaller neighbourhood centres, located in housing estates. Military-style transports should be replaced with marked police cars. More officers should be put on foot patrol.[38] There is some historical evidence that such demilitarisation would be welcomed by the police rank and file.[39] To minimise any risk to the personal safety of police officers, the UK government is entitled to insist that such changes would be carried out only in the context of decommissioning of weapons by the mainstream republican and loyalist paramilitaries. This should not be an insuperable obstacle, as republicans have generally expressed an interest in such all-round decommissioning, and loyalists have said they will turn in their arms if republicans do.

Extensive decommissioning by the major paramilitary organisations, the IRA, the UDA and the UVF, would leave the danger of attacks on the police by small dissident paramilitary groups, and this danger will be highlighted by security-minded politicians opposed to the changes suggested here. The prospects for the survival of these fringe groups, however, will be radically reduced if there is broad acceptance of police reforms. To counter any remaining threat, the police should be allowed resort to arms in particular, and carefully specified, scenarios – as is the case with Great Britain's 'unarmed' police.[40] One possibility would be to allow a small, and separate, unit of the police to retain arms, for use against any group that continues to use violence. The activities of such a unit would have to be carefully monitored, but such a functional division would at least avoid the danger of the entire police service being identified with the excessive use of force.[41]

Any comprehensive reform of the police service must also address the legal environment in which policing operates. Much of the current dissatisfaction with policing, in both loyalist and republican areas, stems from the use of emergency powers, including powers of detention, interrogation and exclusion under the Emergency Provisions Act and the Prevention of Terrorism Act. These laws, and the ways in which they have been abused, have helped to undermine faith in the legal system, and have produced criticism from a number of human rights agencies in Northern Ireland and abroad. It is also clear that they have been less than effective in defeating militant paramilitary organisations over the past thirty years, as Prime Minister Blair recognised in a recent newspaper article.[42] And lastly, while the police have such powers at their disposal, it will be difficult to erode their militaristic ethos and to secure the intake of recruits required to make the police force representative.

There is a very good case, given the current cease-fires, for the emergency laws to be repealed. The argument against, as in the case of disarming, is that some violence and threats of further violence still occur in Northern Ireland, as the Omagh massacre and the events at and occasioned by Drumcree have shown. Some reason that the police must have the powers to respond to any resurgence of large-scale violence. To accept this argument may be self-defeating. An emergency legal regime, involving draconian police powers, inevitably produces excesses by members of the security forces. It may sow dragons' teeth rather than respect for the legal system. Reviewing the legal regime is beyond the scope of the Patten Commission. It is not beyond the remit of the Secretary of State.

Safeguards are required to prevent the legal excesses of the past. The incorporation of the European Convention on Human Rights into British public law is a welcome but limited step. A local Bill of Rights should be put in place which, while permitting government to take the steps necessary to protect society, would make it difficult for legal infringement of civil liberties to take place over a sustained period without extraordinary justification. Precedents for such a Bill of Rights exist in other countries, including the USA, South

Africa and Canada. Police officers, who may be initially opposed to such restrictions on their powers, often come to see the advantages of rights regimes in allowing them to maintain their independence from partisan political control.[43] There is strong support for a comprehensive and modern Bill of Rights among both major communities in Northern Ireland,[44] and there is provision for such rights protection in the Good Friday Agreement.[45]

Conclusion

Nationally impartial policing within a regime of human rights protection is needed if there is to be greater support from nationalists for the police, and a greater likelihood that nationalists will apply to become police officers. Demilitarisation, and the suspension or termination of emergency measures, will have support in loyalist as well as in nationalist circles, but other changes proposed here, including the change to symbols and police membership in the Orange Order and related organisations, will be seen as concessions to nationalists. These are changes, however, which are necessary to make the police nationally as well as religiously or individually impartial. Given the commitment of unionists and the British government in the Good Friday Agreement to the construction of a 'representative' police service, it is incumbent on them and the Patten Commission to take the steps that are necessary to fulfil this promise.

5

Decentralising policing

Centralization easily succeeds in subjecting the external actions of
men to a certain uniformity [and] imparts without difficulty an
admirable regularity to the routine of business; provides skilfully for
the details of the social police; represses small disorders and petty
misdemeanours; maintains society in a status quo alike secure from
improvement and decline; and perpetuates a drowsy regularity in the
conduct of affairs which the heads of administration are wont to call
good order and public tranquillity; in short it excels in prevention,
but not in action.

ALEXIS DE TOCQUEVILLE, *Democracy in America*, vol. ii, p. 90

The RUC has a unitary and centralised administrative structure. It is
a single organisation spanning all of Northern Ireland. It has a single
identity, a single recruitment branch and a single command structure. It is not a complete monolith – it is organised in a number of
territorial divisions – but headquarters sets policy, and local commanders have little discretion. A recruit can be sent anywhere in
Northern Ireland, or be transferred to any other part of it. In practice this has meant that predominantly Catholic regions, such as
south Armagh, or Derry/Londonderry, are mostly policed by
Protestants from outside the region, both in origin and current
residence.

Even if the other reforms advocated in this book were
implemented, the survival of this unitary structure would leave

outstanding problems of legitimacy, democratic accountability, effectiveness and efficiency. A unitary police, even if it were more representative, would have a significant majority of unionist sympathisers in its ranks. There are several districts of Northern Ireland where such a police would be unwelcome in the immediate future. Similarly, many nationalists would be unwilling to serve in a largely unionist police service, particularly if it meant policing beyond the localities in which they live. In consequence a unitary police service would have difficulties in addressing its recruitment composition problem. It would also:

- be unlikely to satisfy the desire of local nationalist (and loyalist) communities to have significant input into the way they are policed; and
- be difficult to reconcile with the Good Friday Agreement's promise to deliver a 'policing service, in constructive and inclusive partnerships with the community at all levels, and with the maximum delegation of authority and responsibility'.

There are two ways to restructure the police to address these problems. The first involves the establishment of a decentralised but still unitary police. The second would involve the formation of a two-tier or federated policing service, which we think would be more in keeping with the Patten Commission's terms of reference and with the spirit of the Good Friday Agreement. In both cases any consistent police reform must ensure that recruitment policies are firmly directed to ensure that Catholics, Protestants and others (and unionists, nationalists and others) are proportionately represented at each level of regional and subregional organisation.

Option 1 – a decentralised single police service

This option involves maintaining the police as a single professional service but would lead to its decentralisation or 'deconcentration' – handing significant operational authority to local commanders, and handing significant power to hold the police to account to local bodies. The RUC has criticised the idea of creating separate two-tier police services, our preferred option, but it has expressed some support for decentralisation in its *Fundamental Review of Policing*, conducted after the first IRA cease-fire of August 1994.

The RUC's review proposed that in the context of a sustained peace, authority in the RUC should be decentralised, with regional commanders being given greater autonomy to make day-to-day operational decisions and to liaise with local Community–Police Liaison Committees (CPLCs). The review recommended that the 'police structure should become more aligned with local communities', and that there should be a 'clearer definition of responsibility' between the regions and headquarters. While maintaining that headquarters should be responsible for establishing 'force policy and standards' and setting the 'strategic direction for the force as a whole', it argued that the regions should be given responsibility for 'disseminating force policy, allocating resources for major policing events and monitoring performance and policing standards'.[1] Unfortunately, the review has only been published in summary form, and it is impossible to know the details of these proposals.

It might be possible to give police headquarters responsibility for those services that are operated most efficiently at a Northern Ireland level, such as personnel and infrastructure services, forensics, recruitment, training and the policing of certain Northern Ireland-wide problems such as drugs, while devolving responsibility for all other matters to local commanders and units. (Headquarters could take responsibility for training in conjunction with the civilian Police Training Agency proposed in Chapter 4.) It might also be possible to give different names to the different regional units of the police and to enable local bodies to whom they are held to account to choose for them differing uniforms and symbols. They should certainly be allowed to vary their titles, or subtitles, to suit local preferences: the unit of the police operating in north Down, for example, could be named the North Down Police or the Northern Ireland Police Service: North Down Department. While retaining a unitary profession it would also be possible to require that the non-senior personnel of each regional unit should be representative of the region's population. And while it would be undesirable, if

not illegal, to restrict membership of the police only to those indigenous to the region, familiarity with the region should be considered a criterion of merit during the recruitment process, as should
an applicant's formal willingness to locate in the area being policed.

Multiple options exist for determining the relevant units of deconcentration. Local police regions could be made coterminous
with:

- the four regional Health and Social Services Boards
- the five Education and Library Boards
- the six counties of Northern Ireland (with, perhaps, city police
  services in Belfast and Derry/Londonderry)
- the twelve current RUC divisions
- the twenty-six local government jurisdictions or
- much smaller jurisdictions, perhaps based on electoral areas or
  wards.

Alternatively, the policing regions could be novel. Since the option
of a decentralised but still unitary police service is not our preferred
option, we have not explored its possible territorial variants in any
further detail.

Option 2 – a two-tier or federal police

A two-tier policing structure, as we use the term, would mark a
radical departure from the status quo. Perhaps we should first say
what it does not mean.[2] It does not mean the present system, in
which the RUC is divided into two components (regulars and reserves), and is involved in two different kinds of policing (of paramilitaries and of 'ordinary' crime). Nor is it what the Chief
Constable means when he proposes the establishment of closer links
between the RUC and local communities.[3] In these organisational
arrangements the police remains a unitary organisation. In our conception of a two-tier policing structure, there would be a number of
separate police services, with one upper-tier police service responsible for all of Northern Ireland, and a number of lower-tier services
responsible for its different regions (graphical illustrations of our

proposals can be found in figures 6.1 and 6.2 on pages 107 and 108). Each of these services would have a different institutional identity, with different names, uniforms and symbols. As with all federal arrangements the two tiers could have exclusive jurisdiction in some matters and joint jurisdiction in others.

Our conception of a two-tier policing structure does not involve the establishment of separate 'ethnic', 'national' or 'communal' police services. Such an arrangement has recently been established in the West Bank and Gaza regions, where there is a Palestinian police responsible for Palestinians, and an Israeli (Jewish) police responsible for policing Jewish settlers. Ethnically based police services also operate in native reservations in North America. These arrangements are appropriate for peoples who have agreed to live separately or who intend to partition their territories. They are not appropriate for the supporters of the Good Friday Agreement.

The federal police services we propose would be organised territorially rather than nationally, ethnically or religiously, but they would be nationally, ethnically and religiously representative of their relevant jurisdictions. This would mean in practice that some districts would have a majority of nationalist or Catholic officers and others a majority of Protestants or unionists. It would be very unlikely that any local service would be homogeneous, unless the level of organisation is as small as that of an electoral ward. In this model it would also be desirable to create matching local institutions, which would hold the police accountable to the local populations. Some of these would have nationalist majorities, some unionist majorities, and others neither. It would also be possible, and in our view desirable, to have a substantial proportion of the local police recruited from the area being policed, because community policing is better carried out by those from the community.[4] This is the practice in several community police services in Europe, notably in Belgium and Switzerland. This territorial restructuring of the police would create a significant number of new openings for police officers from nationalist regions and from working-class loyalist districts. It would also facilitate recruitment among those women who prefer to work close to their homes.

Two-tier policing systems do not currently exist in either Britain or Ireland. The Republic of Ireland has a single unitary police, the Garda Síochána, whereas Britain has several regional police services with none – unless one counts intelligence units – covering the entirety of Great Britain. Ireland itself never had a completely centralised police until the 1920s: Belfast retained its own force until 1865, Derry/Londonderry until 1870, and the Dublin Metropolitan Police (DMP) actually survived until 1925.[5] But multi-tiered systems are widespread elsewhere. They exist throughout much of Europe, and across all of North America.

In the United States, where there is a tradition of distrust of central government that has some resonance in Northern Ireland, the police are organised in at least four tiers. There are, for example, a number of functionally divided federal police services (the best-known of which is the Federal Bureau of Investigation or FBI), and numerous lower-tier police services, for example, state police, municipal police and university campus police. Canada has an asymmetrical federation with a multi-tiered structure of policing. Uniformity is not required of localities. There is a federal police (the Royal Canadian Mounted Police or RCMP), a number of provincial police services, and several municipal police services. Provinces have the choice of providing their own provincial police or contracting with the RCMP, and municipalities have the choice of providing their own services, coalescing with other municipalities to provide a service, or contracting with the provincial police (if one is available) or the RCMP.[6] Canadian arrangements might be considered appropriate for Northern Ireland. Local communities' representatives could be given the right to decide whether to opt for the services of the Northern Ireland Police Service in their locality or to have a separate police service. In this model no local jurisdiction would have a separate lower-tier police foisted on it – each would have the right to opt for one.

There are a number of European and North American states in which policing has been restructured to manage national and ethnic diversity in ways that may be considered pertinent for Northern Ireland. Spanish police police the Basque and Catalan regions of

Spain, but in recognition of these regions' distinct identities they also have their own local forces, the Ertzaintza and Cuerpo Mossos d'Escuadra respectively. Belgium has created a number of local communal police services, in addition to the existing federal gendarmerie and judicial police, which police local French- and Flemish-speaking communities.[7] In Canada, the largely French-speaking province of Quebec has chosen to opt for its own provincial police, the Sûreté du Québec, rather than contract for the services of the federal RCMP. In both Canada and the United States, local police services have been established on reservations in order to address natives' or first nations' requests for a local police.

In many of these cases, the policing tiers are functionally as well as geographically divided, with the lower tier enjoying less extensive powers than its upper-tier counterpart. If such thinking is adopted in Northern Ireland, the local police services could be given responsibility for dealing with relatively minor crimes, such as theft, vandalism and assault. They could be made responsible for child welfare, traffic control, beat patrolling, and increasing community awareness of social problems through school visits. These activities involve the bulk of policing. The Northern Ireland (upper-tier) police could be given responsibility for serious crimes such as rape, murder, drug trafficking, terrorism and public order. Such a division of powers has been recommended by a significant number of individuals in Northern Ireland, including Dr Maurice Hayes, Professor Mike Brogden, Father Raymond Murray and Brian Lennon SJ. It has also been proposed by the SDLP.[8]

One argument behind a functionally divided two-tier service is that nationalists would be more likely to join and embrace a police service that did not have an historical role in security policing, and that was locally based. It could also be cheaper to establish, as lower-tier constables would not need as extensive training programmes, or as much pay, as they would if they performed the full gamut of policing duties. A job in the lower-tier service could also provide the transitional experience needed for a career in the upper-tier police. Given their more limited duties, there would never be a need for the lower-tier police service to be armed or to patrol in intimidating vehicles. Their roles would also mean they would be much less likely to be targeted by recalcitrant or recidivist paramilitaries.

The functional division is not, of course, the sole option. The police services in each tier could be given the same powers. In the Basque area, the Spanish and Basque police have similar powers, and cover the same territory. In the Canadian province of Ontario, local communities choose whether to be policed by provincial or local police. They may even switch from one to the other for a certain period, and then back again.[9] Applied to Northern Ireland this would mean that each region could choose between receiving services from the Northern Ireland Police Service or establishing their own service.

If a two-tier police service is established, one issue that will have to be resolved is the proportion of resources that should go to each tier. This would be affected by the powers assumed by the respective tiers, and by the number of communities that opt to have a local (lower-tier) police service. As we have allocated the bulk of policing duties to the lower-tier police, it seems reasonable that they should be given the bulk of personnel. If lower-tier policing is adopted throughout Northern Ireland and the total number of police officers is kept at 8,000 (for the reasons explained in Chapter 3), we assume that the lower-tier service would need at least 5,000 officers, and the upper tier at most 3,000. The transition to these arrangements would have to be managed in a way that makes all police services representative of the population being policed. While current RUC officers could be expected to make up a high proportion of the upper-tier police, there would also have to be sustained efforts to open the upper tier to more Catholics and nationalists.

As two-tier policing involves a change from the status quo and deals with many nationalist concerns, it should not be surprising that there have been a number of calls for it from nationalists. In its 1995 document *Policing in Northern Ireland*, the SDLP criticised the centralised nature of the Northern Ireland police force and argued for a 'multi-tiered police service organised on a regional basis'.[10] It also called for a distinction to be drawn between 'civilian policing and the type of military role traditionally carried out by the RUC'. In evidence to the Opsahl Commission, a number of representatives of Catholic civil society called for two-tier policing.[11] Sinn Féin proposes, unrealistically, that the RUC should be disbanded and replaced by an all-Ireland police force, but the party has also expressed an interest in an interim 'localised police service/department based on district-council electoral boundaries'.[12]

Such support from nationalists might be considered a 'kiss of death' for these proposals, at least for mainstream unionist politicians. But opinion polls suggest that Catholics, nationalists, Protestants and unionists are open to the concept of two-tier policing. In 1995, 57 per cent of Protestants and 67 per cent of Catholics, representing 61 per cent of all respondents, agreed with the suggestion that the police force should be divided into two 'separate' sections, one of which would deal with 'local policing activities', and the other with major crime including 'anti-terrorist activity'. A further 9 per cent of Protestants and 12 per cent of Catholics were non-committal (see Table 5.1). There is more opposition to this idea among Protestants but there is a cross-community majority in its favour. In December 1997, in response to an independent survey commissioned by the Rowntree Trust, 67 per cent of Catholic respondents maintained that the creation of 'new community policing units separate to the RUC' was either essential (20 per cent), desirable (22 per cent) or acceptable (25 per cent). A slim majority of Protestants (53 per cent) found it essential (4 per cent), desirable (6 per cent), acceptable (24 per cent) or tolerable (19 per cent). In a further question, about 66 per cent of Protestants and about 90 per cent of Catholics found it either essential, desirable, acceptable or tolerable that police accountability should be improved by giving more responsibility for management of police services to 'a number of regional and city police authorities'.[13] Two-tiered policing, in fact, is the only area of substantive policing reform that plainly enjoys cross-community support, which suggests consensual agreement is more likely to be forthcoming on this than on other questions such as the identity (names, symbols, uniforms) of the RUC.

Table 5.1

Public opinion on tiers of policing

Q. *'It has been suggested that the police force be split into two separate sections, one to deal mainly with local policing activities and the other to deal mainly with major crime including anti-terrorist policing. Do you agree or disagree with this suggestion?'*

	PROTESTANTS (N = 1,571)	CATHOLICS (N = 987)	ALL (N = 2,558)
Agree strongly	30	34	32
Agree slightly	27	33	29
Neither agree nor disagree	9	12	10
Disagree slightly	8	7	8
Disagree strongly	26	14	21

Source: Police Authority for Northern Ireland, *Everyone's Police: A Partnership for Change* (Belfast: PANI, 1996), Appendix 6, Table 4.
Note: Don't Knows/Refusals = 0%.

The debate over two-tier policing

A substantial number of political agencies have expressed opposition to two-tier policing. During the parliamentary debate over the Police (Northern Ireland) Bill in December 1997, spokespersons for two of the unionist parties (the UUP and UKUP) attacked the idea of two-tier policing even though the bill did not suggest it.[14] The former Conservative Security Minister, Sir John Wheeler, has also attacked the idea, and the Chief Constable, Ronnie Flanagan, spoke out against it while giving evidence to the parliamentary Northern Ireland Affairs Committee.[15]

One criticism is that two-tier policing is costly and inefficient.[16] Such criticism comes in different forms. There is the argument that Northern Ireland, with only a little over one and a half million people, is too small to have more than one police service, and that the units of a two-tier policing system would not be able to realise the economies of scale that a single unitary police could. As the Chief Constable remarked in evidence to the Northern Ireland Affairs Committee, 'We're much too small a society economically to sustain different police forces.'[17] Related to this is a standard Old

Fabian critique of two-tier structures, including federal systems of government such as those of Canada or Australia. As these involve bureaucratic duplication, the argument goes, they cost more to run than unitary systems.

Comparative public policy analysis demonstrates that communities much smaller than Northern Ireland have their own police services. In North America, even small hamlets often have their own police, as do many university campuses. In Belgium, every local community with at least 10,000 people is entitled to its own police service, and there are 589 formally independent services.[18] If this police-unit-to-population ratio was implemented in Northern Ireland, it would allow for the establishment of over 150 units. Within the UK, the RUC competes in size only with the London Metropolitan Police, which polices over seven million people. Five of Scotland's eight services police areas with less than 400,000 people. Small police services are made possible because of interservice cooperation and help from central government. High-expenditure items, such as training facilities, forensic laboratories or police computer systems, are provided centrally, just as they are in a unitary system.[19] In Britain, for example, where there is a large number of separate regional police services, the central government provides a significant range of services on a national basis, including police colleges and training centres, forensic laboratories and research and development facilities. There is also a Police National Computer at Hendon, to which all police services have access.

While a federated or two-tier service may include some duplication, it is not in fact clear that it is less cost-effective than a single large and monolithic bureaucracy. Competitive pressures work, especially if there is scope for opting in and out of central services, and scope for cost-saving innovations may be greater just because of competition. Two-tier policing may also allow for greater efficiency through functional specialisation, including specialised training: a local police could be trained for community policing, while the upper-tier police could be trained to deal with drugs, terrorism, and whatever other matters came under its jurisdiction. As one policing expert has argued, a community police service requires different skills than those needed by one that polices serious crimes, and it is difficult for a single police service, such as the RUC, to master all these skills simultaneously.[20] There is a last consideration. Whatever costs are incurred in establishing a two-tier policing service have to be weighed against the general economic benefits that would result from creating broadly acceptable policing services. Whatever the alleged efficiency of a centralised unitary service, that has to be weighed against the democratic advantages of creating police services that local communities can identify with and hold accountable.

Another concern is that lower-tier policing would mean 'policing by paramilitaries', as the UUP's security spokesperson Ken Maginnis alleges, or lead to the local police taking 'a more benign view of certain political terrorist activity', as the UKUP's Robert McCartney fears.[21] As we have argued in Chapter 3, the committing of serious human rights abuses should automatically bar anyone from joining the police.[22] There should be no question of handing over the policing role to paramilitary organisations, and current membership of such organisations should be made incompatible with a position in the police. The lower-tier police service would be a formal police service, operating under the rule of law and accountable to representative local political authorities. The goals behind two-tier policing, far from privileging paramilitaries, are twofold:

- to take over the policing of several localities *from* paramilitary organisations, whose present 'policing role' derives its greatest strength from the unacceptability of the RUC, and
- to end punishment beatings and other unacceptable activities.[23]

There is also a fear that lower-tier policing would give rise to the abuse of local minorities by local majorities. The history of local policing in Ireland lends some credence to this fear: the local Belfast police, almost entirely Protestant and 'fiercely anti-Catholic', had to be abolished in 1865 because of their abuse of Catholics.[24] This argument, of course, cuts both ways. There is no obvious reason why a lower-tier police should be any more or less likely to engage in the abuse of minorities than a single unitary police. Under any acceptable policing system, whether federal or unitary, there have to be measures in place to prevent abuse. To that end we have recommended that all police units should be representative of the populations policed,[25] and that it should be illegal to be in the police while a member of any secret or sectarian organisation. We also think that the local police should come under the jurisdiction of the proposed independent ombudsman, although the government might also decide to establish lower-tier ombudsmen, whose decisions could be appealed to the upper-tier level. Local minorities will also be better protected against abuse if the police's emergency powers are scrapped and if a Bill of Rights is adopted that supplements the incorporation of the European Convention on Human Rights into UK domestic law with specific provisions to protect national, religious and ethnic minorities. Last, it should be remembered that an autonomous local police force is not the same as an independent police force. The Secretary of State or the Northern Ireland Assembly – if and when it acquires authority over policing – will retain ultimate authority over the local-tier forces, allowing local police services and oversight agencies flexibility only within centrally established laws and regulations.

Given the likelihood that the upper-tier police would enjoy greater powers than the lower-tier, the greatest dangers to civil liberties are in fact more likely to come from this upper tier rather than from the local policing units. As the Committee for the Administration of Justice has correctly pointed out, the creation of local policing units should not be seen as a substitute for ensuring that the upper-tier police service is properly constrained.[26] Particular attention must be paid to ensure that the upper-tier police are representative and legally as well as democratically accountable.

Another alleged danger of creating more than one police service is that it might lead to inconsistent standards across Northern Ireland, that the different police units might compete, or that they might even clash as in the case of the Palestinian and Israeli forces.[27] We emphasise that all police, regardless of locality, should be required to enforce the same legal code and policing charter: no one in Northern Ireland, unlike in native reserves in North America, is demanding the establishment of different laws for different areas. The prospects of clashes will be minimised if the police (at least the lower tier) are unarmed, if all police services are nationally, religiously and ethnically heterogeneous, and if they are subject to the same overall political authority. None of this applies in the Palestinian–Israeli case, and the clash that occurred there was, so far, an isolated incident. Last, to encourage interservice goodwill it would be prudent if all police officers were trained centrally and if officers were allowed to transfer between different lower-tier services and between the two tiers.

There is also the argument that the creation of local police services would have the effect of entrenching national, religious and ethnic differences when the public policy goal should be to eliminate these. This argument is often put forward by majority groups who oppose local autonomy of any kind for minorities, and by those who want to retain a unitary police force, because they dominate it. We are not persuaded of the merits or the sincerity of this argument. Northern Ireland's divisions are already deeply entrenched. The way to moderate, and eventually to eliminate these divisions is to build up trust between the rival communities over a sustained period. Greater local control over policing, along with the other changes outlined in the Good Friday Agreement, would help Northern Ireland to move in this direction.

Last, civil libertarians have expressed concern that the creation of a lower-tier service alongside an existing one could give rise to a problem of over-policing.[28] This has happened in the Catalan region of Spain, where the lower-tier police was created without any reduction in the size of the already existing Spanish police. However, as we have made clear in our discussion of downsizing in Chapter 3, we envisage a two-tier service involving fewer – not more – police than work in the current single-tier arrangements. We acknowledge, however, that Northern Ireland will need a larger police service than similarly sized regions in the rest of the UK, to facilitate the hiring of Catholic and nationalist officers.

Those persuaded of the case for two-tier policing must converge on one administrative design, even if the relevant design incorporates considerable flexibility. Implementing any two-tier system requires initial agreement on the definition of the tiers. The upper tier is unproblematic: Northern Ireland as a whole. Determining the lower tiers is slightly more problematic. The lower tiers could be built upon any of the following units which are already in existence for certain purposes of public administration:

- the four regional Health and Social Services Boards
- the five Education and Library Boards
- the six counties of Northern Ireland (with, perhaps, city police services in Belfast and Derry/Londonderry)
- the twelve current RUC divisions
- the twenty-six local government jurisdictions or
- smaller jurisdictions, perhaps based on electoral areas, the multi-member units in which local councillors are elected under the Single Transferable Vote, or wards.

The first three of these options either have no obvious policing or community rationale, or lack units of democratic government. The fourth is based on categories that have arisen in the conflict, so there is a strong case for a fresh start for the police and everyone else.

The last two provide the most feasible options from a democratic perspective. We propose that Local Government Districts should be the initial units that are legally required to establish local police services, subject to legal requirements on minimum provision and codes of organisational conduct. We then propose two types of flexibility:

1 We propose that each Local Government District, provided its councillors agree by cross-community consent procedures, should be free to create an amalgamated lower-tier police service with one or more immediately adjacent Local Government Districts.

2 We also propose that the electoral areas used to elect local government councillors should each be entitled either (a) to opt out of the Local Government District police service to establish

its own; (b) to contract with the Northern Ireland Police Service to provide police services in its area; (c) to agree to jointly provide a local service with an adjacent electoral area; or (d) to agree to have its policing service delivered by an immediately adjacent district police service.

We would add some important provisos to this combination of a democratic and quasi-market model: each electoral area should only be able to exercise its opt-out from the Local Government District on the basis of the unanimous consent of its elected councillors, and each could only exercise this option if it had advertised its intention to do so in its personal election address. All these measures would not only have the advantage of satisfying many of Northern Ireland's difficulties with policing, but they would also contribute to the reinvigoration of local government.[29]

In conversations about these ideas, some have objected that Local Government Districts, or electoral areas, are too small as units for policing. We have three initial replies to this objection, and one further thought that should avoid too facile a resolution of this debate. Our three initial replies are: (1) we do not share the 'big is beautiful' philosophy on policing; (2) we know of no compelling cross-national public policy evidence on 'economies of scale' in policing; and (3) we have proposed flexible arrangements for the voluntary amalgamation of service provision by adjacent Local Government Districts. We realise that not everyone will be persuaded by these replies, and we recognise that the issue requires fine judgement. We therefore propose that the onus should be on those persuaded of the merits of larger units for policing services to argue for larger Local Government Districts (and correspondingly larger electoral areas). In our opinion the critical feature of the local tier in federal policing is that it should be plainly attached to existing and elected local governments. We are, for the purposes of this debate, agnostic on whether the existing twenty-six Local Government Districts are of the right size. What must be avoided is a reorganisation of policing that is independent of existing (or future) local government boundaries. In short, any future changes to local government boundaries should have automatic consequences for policing services.

One final administrative observation is in order. Two-tier (Option 2) and decentralised or deconcentrated policing systems (Option 1) are not mutually exclusive. In fact, both systems could be implemented simultaneously. Under this arrangement, the Northern Ireland Police Service – the upper-tier police – would be decentralised, perhaps along the lines suggested by the RUC in its *Fundamental Review of Policing*, while Local Government Districts would be given their own police services to police less serious crimes.

Conclusion

The effect of any of the models described in this chapter should be the same: to hand more control over policing to different localities in Northern Ireland, and to create policing units with which these localities can identify. This approach has several advantages over the status quo. It would make it much more likely that all of Northern Ireland would have formal policing; it would satisfy the demands of local communities – particularly, but not exclusively, nationalist ones – for greater control over policing; and it would be likely to contribute to a higher rate of applications from Catholics and nationalists to become police officers. It is also an approach that has support among both nationalists and unionists.

6

Creating a democratically accountable police service

Sed quis custodiet ipsos custodes? (But who will guard the guardians themselves?)

JUVENAL ON THE PRAETORIAN GUARD OF THE CAESARS, *Satires*, VI, 347–8

In a liberal democracy citizens are sovereign within constitutional constraints: political assemblies are chosen and shaped by citizens; political parties and their candidates are elected by citizens on the basis of public manifestos; and political parties formulate and implement policies for which they are in turn held to account by citizens in regular elections. A democratic assembly may nevertheless agree that certain institutions will be insulated from immediate political control, either by elected politicians or by citizens, for example, the making of interest-rate policies, the decisions of courts, and, indeed, the police's management of some of their operational decisions. Nevertheless, in liberal democracies it is citizens, albeit within constitutional constraints, who can and should in principle determine what degree of freedom any such institutions should have from immediate accountability to the assembly.

Police must be accountable in democracies in two senses, according to Geoffrey Marshall:[1] (1) the subordinate or obedient sense, and (2) the explanatory and co-operative sense. In the first sense police must necessarily be subject to someone's, or some institution's, administrative control and power to direct and veto. Usually the most senior police officer or prosecutor is such a supervisor. It is the second sense that raises questions of formal political accountability. Senior police officers necessarily make policy in protecting the law because their resources are limited and they must direct police officers' priorities. Such policy-making must, in a democratic order, be held to account, either directly by the relevant assembly itself, or by one of its subcommittees, or by a body delegated with that authority by the assembly.

In a nationally divided region, especially one in which the police have historically been associated with one particular ethnic or national community, citizens require assurances that the police are all the people's police, and democratic inputs and democratic evaluations of police outputs should be as inclusive as possible. Any delegated institution charged with holding the police to account must therefore be representative of all the relevant national communities, and have decision-making rules that prevent one community's representatives from imposing its wishes on the others. Within any such framework it is desirable, and indeed essential, that police professionals should be allowed to operate in particular cases without political interference – although citizens and their parties should be able to hold the police accountable for their policies in pursuing crime, and for their efficiency. These are the institutional ideals that we moderns invoke to answer the dilemma of the Caesars. It is we, the citizens, who guard the guards, by subordinating them to the law and by holding their senior officers to account.

Ideals and realities

These are sensible democratic ideals. They are also feasible ideals. They are not utopian aspirations. The current situation in Northern Ireland falls considerably short of all of them. A member of the British government – the Secretary of State for Northern Ireland – who is not elected, even indirectly, by the citizens of Northern

Ireland holds executive power over the RUC. The power to legislate on policing matters is a prerogative of the Westminster parliament – in which Northern Irish MPs comprise 1 MP for every 37 MPs from Great Britain. The new Northern Ireland Assembly has, as yet, no responsibility for security or policing.

The Police Authority for Northern Ireland has since 1970 had the task of holding the police to account on behalf of Northern Ireland's citizens. It is widely regarded as ineffective. It is not representative, and it makes its decisions by simple majority vote. It is a quasi-non-governmental organisation, a quango. It is not an elected body. It is not an indirectly elected body. It is appointed by the Secretary of State on the advice of her unelected officials. Some districts of Northern Ireland have local Community–Police Liaison Committees that seek to influence policing on a local level, but they have no formal powers, and most ordinary citizens with whom we have discussed these issues are, unsurprisingly, unaware of their existence.

The status quo: an election-free zone

The Secretary of State sets the policing budget and, in co-operation with the Chief Constable of the RUC and the British Army GOC (Northern Ireland), plays a key role in establishing security policy. She is the main person, in consultation with her cabinet colleagues, responsible for legislative changes that affect policing. For these reasons, among others, the future of police accountability, whatever the outcome of the Patten Commission, will ultimately depend on the decisions of the Secretary of State and her colleagues.

The legislation establishing the Police Authority stipulated that, as far as practicable, it should be representative of the community. The Police Authority was charged with providing an 'efficient and effective' police force, and was given direct responsibility for a number of aspects of policing, including the hiring and disciplining of senior officers, from Assistant Chief Constable upwards. It has had responsibilities in the allocation of expenditure on policing, and in the maintenance of police buildings and the provision of supplies – although much of this responsibility has been transferred to the Chief Constable under the recent Police (Northern Ireland) Act 1998. It was hoped that the Police Authority would act as a buffer between the Secretary of State, any devolved government and the Chief Constable, to protect the operational independence of the latter.

The legislation was partly aimed at bringing policing arrangements in Northern Ireland closer to those implemented in Great Britain by the Police and Magistrates Courts Act (1964). This administrative harmonisation would not have occurred so quickly had it not been for the riots and pogroms of 1969 – in which the police were directly implicated. The Hunt Report argued that the UUP had exercised partisan control over the RUC and that Catholics had little confidence in the police's impartiality. Hunt's answer was professionalisation on the British model, and the establishment of a representative Police Authority. The reforms implemented, however, did not import any British model, lock, stock and barrel. Police Authorities in Scotland are composed entirely of elected councillors, while those in England and Wales have a majority of elected councillors. The members of Northern Ireland's Police Authority are, by contrast, appointed by the Secretary of State. This procedure was established despite Hunt's express recommendation that the Police Authority should be elected, and was justified on the grounds that it was necessary to prevent the politicisation of policing.

Since its inception the Police Authority has opted for a low profile. Until recently, it met in secret. Its membership and most of what it did were unknown to the public it was representing. It has been almost completely uncritical, claiming in a 1989 report that the RUC was 'one of the best police forces in the world',[2] a pronouncement that we are certain was not based on anything resembling comparative public policy research. Rather than representing the community to the police, it has appeared more interested in representing the police to the community.[3] The Police Authority has confined its attention, for the most part, to largely mundane technical and administrative matters, such as the provision of police supplies, equipment and buildings.[4] There has been no noticeable attempt by it to change or even investigate controversial police policies such as the use of supergrasses, illegal interrogation methods at various 'holding centres', the deployment of undercover units, and the firing of plastic bullets at unarmed demonstrators.[5] There have been no public inquiries by the Police Authority into weighty (and sometimes palpably accurate) allegations of collusion between the RUC and loyalist paramilitaries, of a shoot-to-kill policy against republican militants in the 1980s, or, more recently, of the intimidation and worse of lawyers who defend republican clients.

The Police Authority's failure to represent citizens' concerns, and to hold the RUC to account, is reflected in its own survey data. Less than half of all respondents are aware that the Police Authority and the RUC are independent organisations.[6] The unwillingness of the Police Authority members to brook even moderate criticism of the police was graphically illustrated in 1996.[7] Two members of the Police Authority, Chris Ryder and David Cook, who objected publicly to the flying of the Union Jack over police stations on unionist holidays, and to the fact that police recruits had to swear allegiance to the Queen, were censured by a majority of the Police Authority's members. They were subsequently ejected from the Police Authority. Neither member was particularly outspoken by nature, nor could either be described as nationalist. Cook has been a leading light in the Alliance Party, and Ryder is the author of a history of the RUC in which he expresses his 'limitless admiration' for its 'courage and professionalism'.[8] In one author's threefold typology of pro-RUC, neutral and anti-RUC literature, Ryder's book is listed in the pro-RUC category,[9] a judgement with which any reader will concur.

The Police Authority's weakness has multiple causes. Paramilitary violence encouraged the Police Authority to be secretive. Two of its members were murdered, and a third was forced to resign after being named as a target by the IRA. Police casualty rates, and the need to maintain police morale, contributed to a reluctance among the Police Authority's members to criticise the RUC openly. Republican violence led the RUC to resist any interference in its activities by civilian agencies. It was, in Ryder's words, 'a force under fire', and its Police Authority reacted accordingly. Political violence also increased governmental and unionist hostility towards stronger accountability mechanisms, lest these obstruct 'the fight against terrorism'. They were happy to have a Police Authority with no authority.

There is a notion that a tripod governs the RUC: a 'partnership' of the Police Authority, the Secretary of State and the Chief Constable. It is a risible notion. If it is a tripod it is one with a missing leg. The Police Authority is that missing leg. It has been shut out of the formulation of security policy. Its members are appointed by the Secretary of State. She appoints its Chair and vice-Chair. The Secretary of State can sack its members, as Sir Patrick Mayhew sacked Cook and Ryder in 1996. The Police Authority's powers in relation to the Chief Constable have not been defined clearly, and he has been able to insist on a very broad interpretation of the doctrine of 'operational independence'.[10] On those occasions on which the RUC hierarchy and the Police Authority have disagreed, the latter 'has rarely been able to prevail over the RUC'.[11] The former RUC Chief Constable Hugh Annesley explained to the Northern Ireland Committee of the Irish Congress of Trade Unions that he would be likely to pay as much attention to the Police Authority as to a letter in the *Irish News* (Northern Ireland's main nationalist newspaper).[12] It is difficult to construe this remark as complimentary to either the Police Authority or the *Irish News*. The Police Authority even manages to condemn itself in its own submissions to the House of Commons.[13]

The members of the Police Authority, whether Catholic or Protestant, have tended to be deferential towards the police. They have not generally asserted the powers they do possess, such as the power to call for reports, or to control supplies of equipment, such as plastic bullets,[14] or insisted on more radical powers. In the words of one former member, they have behaved more like a 'performing poodle than an effective watchdog'.[15] This deference flows, in part, from the fact that the body is government-appointed.[16] Not only is this government British, it has been Conservative for twenty-two of the last thirty years. Conservative appointees continue to dominate the Police Authority, despite Labour's landslide victory in 1997.[17] The deference can be attributed to the fact that the SDLP and, less importantly, the Northern Ireland Committee of the Irish Congress of Trade Unions have refused to take seats on the Police Authority. This unwillingness in turn flows largely from the Police Authority's weak powers, its majoritarian decision-making rules, and the absence, until recently, of an overall political settlement. Sinn Féin has had no representation on the Police Authority, because it has not been invited to take any places, and in any case would be unwilling to participate.

The Police Authority's current composition underlines the problem of (foolishly or deliberately?) confusing religious and national identity in Northern Ireland, and the illogic of trying to resolve the problem of a nationally divided region simply by treating religious groups fairly. The Police Authority is 'representative' of Northern Ireland's religious diversity. Indeed it has been suggested that it may have slightly more Catholic than Protestant members. But the Catholics who participate in the Police Authority can hardly be considered representative of *nationalist* opinion.[18] They have been described to us as 'Uncle Toms and Aunty Thomasinas'. The 1970 Police Act did not stipulate that 'representative' should mean 'representative of nationalists, unionists and others'. Instead it stipulated that the Police Authority should be broadly representative of a number of interests, like agriculture, commerce, industry, universities, the legal professions etcetera. In consequence Pat Armstrong, Chair of the Police Authority, in giving evidence to the Northern Ireland Affairs Committee was able to claim that 'on paper we are broadly representative'.[19]

Because of its timidity and its composition, nationalists do not see the Police Authority as an effective institution, or as impartial between unionists and nationalists. Militant republicans, by contrast, consider it 'an integral part of the British apparatus of repression'.[20] In the view of Dr Maurice Hayes, a respected non-partisan, there is a 'total lack of faith' among Catholics 'in the Police Authority as a means of ensuring public accountability'.[21] The low esteem in which nationalists hold the Police Authority was indicated by a storm in February 1998 over government appointments to the new Parades Commission. The government appointed two working-class loyalists with solid paramilitary connections, but two middle-class Catholics without nationalist credentials. The most frequent accusation levelled against one of the Catholics by nationalists was that she had been a member of the Police Authority.[22]

Community–Police Liaison Committees

Since the 1980s, a number of local Community–Police Liaison Committees (CPLCs) have been established in Northern Ireland similar to those suggested by Lord Scarman for England and Wales after the Brixton riots of 1981. They are supposed to ensure that 'policing decisions are in tune with the needs of local people' and to 'improve relations between the police and public'.[23] The committees have no statutory basis or powers and have developed largely as a result of local initiative, and in an uneven and piecemeal fashion.[24] By 1998, Northern Ireland had thirty-nine CPLCs. Sixteen of these were concentrated in the Greater Belfast region while there were none in Newry or south Armagh, and only one in County Fermanagh.[25]

An in-depth study of seventeen of these committees was undertaken in 1990 by an American academic, Ronald Weitzer. He concluded that the committees suffered from a number of major shortcomings similar to those of the Police Authority.[26] Meetings of the CPLCs, like those of the Police Authority, were normally closed to the public that they were supposed to represent – despite a Home Office circular that a 'group can only command the confidence of the local community if its meetings are in general open to press and public'. In eleven CPLCs, meetings had never been publicised. The secretiveness of these meetings might lead one to suspect that controversial security policies, such as sectarian attacks or the routing of marches, were being discussed. It was not so. The committees tended to focus on mundane policing issues, such as traffic problems, teenage drinking, vandalism, and street lighting. This was the case whether they were located in quiet or intensely troubled regions. The CPLCs were generally uncritical and deferential. Several members supported a programme to have laypersons carry out spot checks on how detainees were held in police stations, not to protect the detainees, but to dispel 'propaganda about ill-treatment by the RUC'. The CPLCs were not broadly representative. They were dominated by unionists, and by the UUP in particular. Fourteen of the CPLCs examined by Weitzer were chaired by unionists, and a further two by members of the Alliance Party. The SDLP and Sinn Féin boycott the committees. The members of the CPLCs are middle class, with little experience of police–community conflict in working-class republican or loyalist districts. Not surprisingly, Weitzer concluded that the committees had a limited impact on police–community relations, and on police accountability. This conclusion was borne out by a survey conducted for the Police Authority in late 1997: 62 per cent of respondents (59 per cent of Protestants and 67 per cent of Catholics) said they were not aware of the existence of the CPLCs.[27]

Holding the police to account

The Westminster government appears to be aware that the Police Authority and the CPLCs have serious shortcomings. The Police (Northern Ireland) Act 1998 seeks to strengthen accountability by clarifying the relationship between the Police Authority, the Chief Constable and the Secretary of State. The act makes the Police Authority responsible for drawing up an annual policing plan, and requires it to seek input from the community, including the elected district councils. Whether the act will strengthen the Police Authority is another question. The Chief Constable's operational independence remains undefined. The act transfers much of the control over expenditures on policing and the provision of supplies from the Police Authority to the Chief Constable. The Committee for the Administration of Justice argues that this may weaken the Police Authority, depriving it of a 'potentially very powerful tool of control'.[28]

The government has also recently released a consultation document, *Your Voice, Your Choice*. It discusses ways in which community participation in policing might be enhanced through changes to the Police Authority and the CPLCs.[29] The document asks whether the Police Authority should continue to be appointed as at present, or elected, or partly elected and partly appointed. It questions whether it should be regionally based, and whether an elected or appointed Police Authority should be given the power to elect its own chairman and vice-chairman – a power currently vested in the Secretary of State. It also asks if CPLCs should be established on a statutory basis – with one in each district council, whether there should be statutory lines of communication from them to the police and the Police Authority, and how they should be constituted.

These leading suggestions would represent improvements over the status quo. An elected police authority, possessed of a democratic mandate, would be a more legitimate and less timid body than the current authority. It would be more likely to assert its powers, and to press for new ones.[30] But to avoid the near certainty of a nationalist boycott the government would have to implement a host of other substantial changes along the lines suggested elsewhere in this book. It would also have to ensure that the new elected Police Authority is not a majoritarian institution, but has provisions to protect minorities against policies they do not want.[31] Nationalist participation is more likely if the powers of the Police Authority are considerably widened at the outset. A change in its name might help mark a formal break with the past, for example, to the Northern Ireland Police Committee (NIPC).

The CPLCs should be formally established in each district council. To ensure that they are representative of their communities, they should either be directly elected, through the single transferable vote (STV), or be indirectly elected from the local district councillors, or appointed by political parties in proportion to their electoral strength in all the relevant districts. This need not rule out participation by individuals without party connections, or by representatives of civil society associations, providing they are nominated by elected politicians or run as independents. If direct elections are

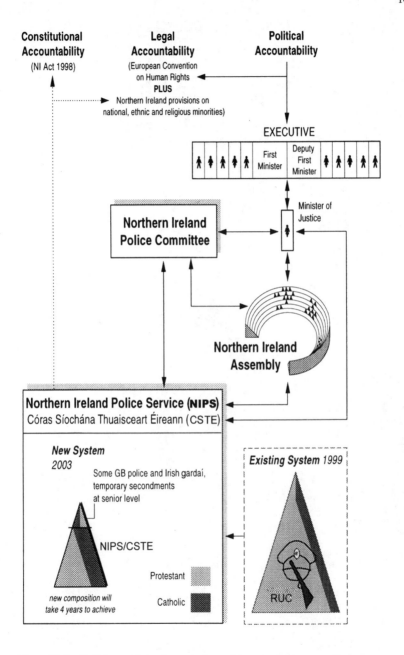

Figure 6.1 Policing with justice, security and human rights: upper tier

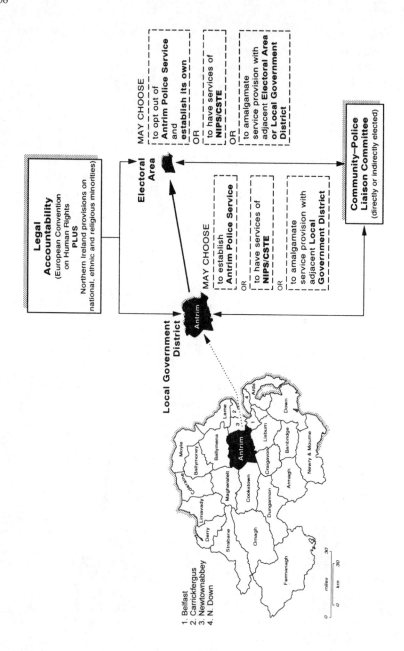

Figure 6.2 Policing with justice, security and human rights: lower tier

preferred, as we think they should be, these must take place on the same day as district council elections, to cut costs and to help ensure a reasonable turnout.[32] Elections to multiple democratic institutions, for example, police boards, library boards and local councils, are the norm in North America.

The CPLCs' meetings should be open, and they should be obliged to consult with their local communities over policing priorities.[33] They should be given defined statutory responsibility to help shape general police policy and priorities, and this should apply to the full range of police activities, not just mundane issues such as traffic control or petty burglaries. Local police commanders should be required to consult with them, to appear before them when requested, and to take their recommendations into account.[34] The CPLCs should have input into the deliberations of whatever Northern Ireland-wide institutions are created to control the police. One way to organise a new Northern Ireland Police Committee, in fact, would be to constitute it as a federal body, with its membership drawn from the new CPLCs.

If a two-tier police service is adopted, each CPLC should be mandated with ensuring that its local police service is effective, nationally impartial, and representative of the local population, and should be responsible for naming the local force, and for the design of its symbols and uniforms. The CPLCs should collectively be given responsibilities for administering the local policing budget, and for the hiring and firing of senior officers. To prevent abuse, certain decisions of a CPLC, such as the firing of local commanders, should be capable of being appealed to a newly constituted Northern Ireland Police Committee of the Assembly and the courts.

Any conceivable strengthening of the Police Authority and the CPLCs, however, would still leave the most important powers over policing in the hands of the Secretary of State and the Westminster parliament. The latest Police Act which, among other things, establishes a Police Ombudsman for Northern Ireland and changes the oath that police officers must take, was passed at Westminster. While it aims at increasing the accountability of the police by requiring the Police Authority to draft annual policing plans, it also gives a range of new powers to the Secretary of State, including the powers to issue a code of practice to the Police Authority, to issue guidance to the Chief Constable about policing, to require the police to use certain equipment, and to establish new organisations to conduct research into the police's efficiency and effectiveness.

The only way, in our view, to make the police properly democratically accountable to the people of Northern Ireland is to transfer legislative and executive control over policing to the Northern Ireland Assembly and a new Ministry of Justice. This should be done at the end of the two-year transitional period that began with the Good Friday Agreement. To allay concerns, and to act as an incentive to paramilitaries to hand in their weapons, any such transfer of power should be conditional on verifiable decommissioning by all mainstream paramilitary organisations.

Two objections generally arise to the idea of transferring executive and legislative control over policing to Northern Ireland's politicians. The first recalls the way in which they abused this power in the past. Unionists in the Stormont regime used their control over policing to disastrous partisan effect. This abuse led to the establishment of a police authority and partly accounted for the abolition of the Stormont regime. For this reason, nationalists have traditionally been wary of allowing elected local institutions to have control over policing. Martin McGuinness of Sinn Féin argued recently that giving elected politicians control over policing would be a 'non-starter' as unionists would dominate such arrangements.[35] Ironically, senior RUC officers and the Police Authority share his views: they argue that greater policing powers for Northern Ireland politicians would open the door 'to partisan political control'.[36]

This thinking can be transcended. Majoritarian decision-making does allow a majority to monopolise power. Things need not be so. The decision-making rules in the new Northern Ireland Assembly are based on consensus, and it is now impossible to pass legislation on key decisions that does not have the approval of sizeable components of the unionist and nationalist blocs, as well as a majority overall.[37] Other safeguards can be used to ensure that the holder of the policing portfolio has substantial cross-community support. As the First Minister and Deputy First Minister are required to have significant cross-community support for their election, control over policing could be given to either of them, or both.

Those concerned that the devolution of control over policing will lead to partisanship overlook the extent to which current arrangements are nationally partisan. Currently, control over policing lies largely with the British parliament and government. This may be better than arrangements under the Stormont regime, but it can hardly be considered neutral. The Police Authority has little or no representation from nationalists, and it has failed to criticise the police or to investigate nationalist complaints against the police.[38] Its members have no mandate from the people of Northern Ireland, including its nationalist community. They are appointed by a *British* Secretary of State. Our proposals, by contrast, would empower both local nationalists and local unionists, and give them incentives to engage in co-operative policy-making.

The second potential criticism of our proposal can now be anticipated: it suggests that the devolution of control over policing would lead to interminable bickering and failure to reach agreement. This is a pessimistic assumption, one that emanates from the same minds that predicted that there would be no overall political agreement in Northern Ireland. It is also the kind of criticism that is levelled against any power-sharing arrangement, given that they, by their very nature, require agreement between disparate groups.

This problem is not a compelling argument against power-sharing. It is a reason for designing institutions with incentives to prevent disagreements, and default mechanisms that limit the damage caused by them. While unionists and nationalist politicians may be under pressure from radicals within their own bloc to disagree on policing, they will also be under pressure to agree, because agreement will underpin stability and facilitate co-operation on non-policing matters.[39] Default mechanisms can be built in if it is considered vital to prevent deadlock. If consensus cannot be reached on a particular policing matter, it might be referred upwards to the British government, acting in co-operation with its Irish counterpart through the intergovernmental conference. Giving the British government the final say in such an appeal will give nationalists in the Assembly additional incentives to work towards compromise with their unionist colleagues. Giving the Irish government an important role should create a similar incentive for unionists. In the worst-case scenarios, control of policing could be taken away from the Assembly and handed over to the British and Irish governments, although we doubt that this will be necessary.

If it is accepted that control over policing should be devolved to the Northern Ireland Assembly and executive, the task of overseeing the police and the ministry responsible for policing could fall to a committee of the Assembly rather than to a separate police authority/committee. Under the Good Friday Agreement, all committees have scrutiny, policy development and consultation roles with respect to the departments with which each is associated. They also have the power to consider and advise on annual plans, to call individuals to give evidence or conduct research, to initiate inquiries and to make reports. Committees are proportionately constituted, and their recommendations on legislation are subject to the cross-community consent procedure in the Assembly at large. As an additional safeguard, it should be stipulated that the Policing Committee should be headed by a politician from a different party than the minister responsible for policing.

While the transfer of executive and legislative control over policing to the Northern Ireland Assembly might obviate the need for a separate Northern Ireland-wide police authority, there would still be a need for strong and democratic local bodies to oversee policing at a community level. Northern Ireland's communities are too diverse to be fairly represented by centralised institutions. Local institutions would be especially necessary if a two-tier police structure is adopted, but would still be needed even if it is not.

Are these democratic opinions out of line with public opinion? Survey information on these questions is vague and limited, but what there is suggests some popular support for our arguments. A poll conducted in Northern Ireland just before the Good Friday Agreement indicated that 74 per cent of Protestants and 87 per cent of Catholics thought it was either 'essential', 'desirable', 'acceptable' or 'tolerable' to improve accountability of policing by transferring more responsibility to a new 'Department of Justice and Northern Ireland Assembly'. A clear majority of both Protestants and Catholics also found it essential, desirable, acceptable or tolerable to give additional responsibilities to 'a number of regional and city Police Authorities'.[40]

A last word on accountability. Policing in England and Wales, and Northern Ireland has always had one feature that astonishes legalists, democrats and constitutionalists elsewhere in Europe and in North America. The independent power of the police to prosecute suspects as well as to arrest them has multiple undesirable consequences. It enables unscrupulous street-level police to use the threat of prosecution as a form of harassment that is difficult to check. Making the police the initial judges of the legal merits of their work means that prosecution cases may be insufficiently scrutinised, and that due process in investigations may be insufficiently protected. And at the most senior levels these arrangements may encourage tacit collusion among the insufficiently separated policing and legal authorities. Things need not be like this, and indeed such arrangements are not intrinsic to British institutions. The separation of policing from prosecution is a feature of one legal jurisdiction in Great Britain: Scotland's. We believe that a procurator fiscal on the Scottish model – or district attorney on the US model – should have a monopoly of public power to prosecute cases before the courts. Judicial oversight of due process would be better protected under these arrangements and the (perceived as well as actual) capacity of the police to abuse the power of prosecution would be removed – thereby enhancing the legitimacy of the new police services.

Conclusion

The institutions currently responsible for holding the RUC accountable to the people of Northern Ireland, the Police Authority and local Community–Police Liaison Committees, are widely and rightly regarded as failures. This view is shared by the British government, if only implicitly, and it has called for suggestions on how they should be reformed. Even if the Police Authority and the CPLCs are given more power and made more democratic, the Westminster government and parliament would continue to exercise ultimate legislative and executive control over policing. We believe that this 'remote control' is no longer necessary given the emergence of a power-sharing government with strong institutional protections for minorities. We have therefore argued that the Secretary of State's powers over policing should be transferred to the Northern Ireland Assembly and government – something that Northern Irish politicians can request under the terms of the Good Friday Agreement.

Our argument for reform is concluded. We have argued for nationally representative police, for police services that are nationally impartial, for a federal or two-tier territorial structure, and for properly democratic arrangements to hold the new police services to account. Our proposals take into account the interests, identities and ideas of unionists, nationalists and others. They are guided by the history of policing in Ireland and by comparative knowledge of national and ethnic conflicts elsewhere. Our argument is consistent with the terms of reference of the Patten Commission and the letter and spirit of the Good Friday Agreement. It is fully consistent with the new consociational and confederal arrangements endorsed by the people of Northern Ireland. It meets the minority and human rights tests established in the Agreement. It provides benchmarks against which the recommendations of the Patten Commission can be judged.[41] We hope that the publication of the Patten Commission's report and the UK government's response to it will ensure that there will be no need to write a second edition of this book.

Appendix A
Police reform in the
Good Friday Agreement*

Policing and justice

1 The participants [in the British–Irish Agreement] recognise that policing is a central issue in any society. They equally recognise that Northern Ireland's history of deep divisions has made it highly emotive, with great hurt suffered and sacrifices made by many individuals and their families, including those in the RUC and other public servants. They believe that the agreement provides the opportunity for a new beginning to policing in Northern Ireland with a police service capable of attracting and sustaining support from the community as a whole. They also believe that this agreement offers a unique opportunity to bring about a new political dispensation which will recognise the full and equal legitimacy and worth of the identities, senses of allegiance and ethos of all sections of the community in Northern Ireland. They consider that this opportunity should inform and underpin the development of a police service representative in terms of the make-up of the community as a whole and which, in a peaceful environment, should be routinely unarmed.

2 The participants believe it essential that policing structures and arrangements are such that the police service is professional,

effective and efficient, fair and impartial, free from partisan political control; accountable, both under the law for its actions and to the community it serves; representative of the society it polices, and operates within a coherent and co-operative criminal justice system, which conforms with human rights norms. The participants also believe that those structures and arrangements must be capable of maintaining law and order including responding effectively to crime and to any terrorist threat and to public order problems. A police service which cannot do so will fail to win public confidence and acceptance. They believe that any such structures and arrangements should be capable of delivering a policing service, in constructive and inclusive partnerships with the community at all levels, and with the maximum delegation of authority and responsibility, consistent with the foregoing principles. These arrangements should be based on principles of protection of human rights and professional integrity and should be unambiguously accepted and actively supported by the entire community.

3 An independent Commission will be established to make recommendations for future policing arrangements in Northern Ireland including means of encouraging widespread community support for these arrangements within the agreed framework of principles reflected in the paragraphs above and in accordance with the terms of reference at Annex A. The Commission will be broadly representative with expert and international representation among its membership and will be asked to consult widely and to report no later than Summer 1999.

4 The participants believe that the aims of the criminal justice system are to:

- deliver a fair and impartial system of justice to the community;
- be responsive to the community's concerns, and encouraging community involvement where appropriate;
- have the confidence of all parts of the community; and
- deliver justice efficiently and effectively.

5 There will be a parallel wide-ranging review of criminal justice (other than policing and those aspects of the system relating to the

emergency legislation) to be carried out by the British Government through a mechanism with an independent element, in consultation with the political parties and others. The review will commence as soon as possible, will include wide consultation, and a report will be made to the Secretary of State no later than Autumn 1999. Terms of Reference are attached at Annex B [not included in this Appendix].

6 Implementation of the recommendations arising from both reviews will be discussed with the political parties and with the Irish Government.

7 The participants also note that the British Government remains ready in principle, with the broad support of the political parties, and after consultation, as appropriate, with the Irish Government, in the context of ongoing implementation of the relevant recommendations, to devolve responsibility for policing and justice issues.

Annex A
Commission on Policing for Northern Ireland

Terms of Reference

Taking account of the principles on policing as set out in the agreement, the Commission will inquire into policing in Northern Ireland and, on the basis of its findings, bring forward proposals for future policing structures and arrangements, including means of encouraging widespread community support for those arrangements. Its proposals on policing should be designed to ensure that policing arrangements, including composition, recruitment, training, culture, ethos and symbols, are such that in a new approach Northern Ireland has a police service that can enjoy widespread support from, and is seen as an integral part of, the community as a whole.

Its proposals should include recommendations covering any issues such as re-training, job placement and educational and professional development required in the transition to policing in a peaceful society.

Its proposals should also be designed to ensure that:

- the police service is structured, managed and resourced so that it can be effective in discharging its full range of functions (including proposals on any necessary arrangements for the transition to policing in a normal peaceful society);
- the police service is delivered in constructive and inclusive partnerships with the community at all levels with the maximum delegation of authority and responsibility;
- the legislative and constitutional framework requires the impartial discharge of policing functions and conforms with internationally accepted norms in relation to policing standards;
- the police operate within a clear framework of accountability to the law and the community they serve, so:
  - they are constrained by, accountable to and act only within the law;
  - their powers and procedures, like the law they enforce, are clearly established and publicly available;
  - there are open, accessible and independent means of investigating and adjudicating upon complaints against the police;
  - there are clearly established arrangements enabling local people, and their political representatives, to articulate their views and concerns about policing and to establish publicly policing priorities and influence policing policies, subject to safeguards to ensure police impartiality and freedom from partisan political control;
  - there are arrangements for accountability and for the effective, efficient and economic use of resources in achieving policing objectives;
  - there are means to ensure independent professional scrutiny and inspection of the police service to ensure that proper professional standards are maintained;
- the scope for structured co-operation with the Garda Siochana and other police forces is addressed; and
- the management of public order events which can impose

exceptional demands on policing resources is also addressed.

The Commission should focus on policing issues, but if it identifies other aspects of the criminal justice system relevant to its work on policing, including the role of the police in prosecution, then it should draw the attention of the Government to those matters.

The Commission should consult widely, including with non-governmental expert organisations, and through such focus groups as they consider it appropriate to establish.

The Government proposes to establish the Commission as soon as possible, with the aim of it starting work as soon as possible and publishing its final report by Summer 1999.

Appendix B
Summary

1 The RUC has not in the past and does not now meet the terms of reference of the Independent Commission on Policing.
2 The RUC's history, under the previous devolved government, and under direct rule, has made it widely and deeply unacceptable among Catholics and nationalists. It also has legitimacy problems with loyalists and in working-class districts.
3 Any new police service(s) should be nationally representative. The UK government should set itself the target of increasing the proportion of Catholics in the police to 40 per cent within four years. For now, the goal of increasing representativeness should be placed higher than the goal of 'downsizing'.
4 To ensure full impartiality and to encourage nationalists to join the police service(s) they should be made nationally impartial. Neutral or bi-national names, symbols and codes of conduct are imperative.
5 The new Northern Ireland-wide police service should be called (in English) the Northern Ireland Police Service and (in Gaelic) Córas Síochána Thuaisceart Éireann.
6 A policing charter for all services should make clear that police officers, in the conduct of their duties, must be neutral between unionists, nationalists and others, and that unionists, nationalists

and others are welcome to join the police service(s).

7 Police service(s) should be normalised and de-militarised. Most police should not be routinely armed. Super-barracks should be phased out in favour of smaller local stations. Training should be placed under the control of a civilian Police Training Agency. The police service(s) should operate under normal rather than emergency legislation. The police should lose their power of independent prosecution.

8 Police service(s) should be decentralised in a federal manner (see figures 6.1 and 6.2, pages 107 and 108). The Northern Ireland Police Service/Córas Síochána Thuaisceart Éireann should have (upper-tier) Northern Ireland-wide jurisdiction. Lower-tier police service(s) should also be established, initially within Local Government Districts – they should be entitled to opt to contract to have the services of the Northern Ireland Police Service/Córas Síochána Thuaisceart Éireann, or to amalgamate police provision with adjacent districts. Federal policing will make it easier to create representative and impartial police service(s); it will make it easier to have a fresh start; it will provide policing sensitive to local conditions and needs; and it will encourage efficiency and innovation. All policing units would be governed by the same legal standards, and their political overseers would be required to maintain minimum services.

9 The new police service(s) should be legally and democratically accountable. The government should proceed with the establishment of a strong and independent Ombudsman, perhaps backed by local ombudspersons. The UK government and the Northern Ireland Assembly should proceed rapidly to create a special Bill of Rights, one that protects national, ethnic and religious minorities, to complement the European Convention on Human Rights.

10 The government should replace the Northern Ireland Police Authority and local Community–Police Liaison Committees with a new Northern Ireland Police Committee and corresponding local bodies. The new bodies should be elected (directly or indirectly), or appointed by elected Northern Ireland

politicians, either in the Assembly or in Local Government Districts. They should have effective powers to shape general policing policy and to hold police service(s) to account. They should be elected (directly or indirectly) under rules of proportional representation and they should conduct their business according to cross-community consent procedures.

Notes

Introduction

1 Frank Wright, 'Northern Ireland and the British–Irish relationship', *Studies*, 78 (1989): pp. 151–62.

1 A police that is not everyone's

* Our chapter heading is a counter-suggestive response to the 1995 survey report commissioned and published by the Police Authority for Northern Ireland, *Everyone's Police: A Partnership for Change* (Belfast: PANI, 1996).
1 The Northern Ireland Affairs Committee, *Composition, Recruitment and Training of the RUC*, Vol. II, *Minutes of Evidence and Appendices* (London: Stationery Office, 1998), p. 45.
2 Alex Maskey, 'Current police force no good for the new era', *Irish News*, Belfast, 19 May 1998. See also 'Republicans demand creation of new police service', *Irish News*, Belfast, 5 June 1998.
3 Anthony MacIntyre, cited in *Policing in a New Society* (Belfast: Centre for Research and Documentation, 1994), p. 40.
4 According to the RUC's official estimation, 7.5 per cent of all RUC officers are Catholic. Catholics represent 8.2 per cent of 'regular' RUC officers, 6.9 per cent of the full-time Reserve, and 4.8 per cent of the part-time Reserve. Figures from Northern Ireland Affairs Committee, *Composition, Recruitment and Training of the RUC*, p. 14.
5 SDLP, *Policing in Northern Ireland*

(Belfast: SDLP, 1995), p. 8.
6 *House of Commons Hansard Debates*, London, 15 December 1997, cols. 49 and 73.
7 Ibid., cols. 52–3. The UUP's security spokesperson, Ken Maginnis, approvingly cited Leslie Rodgers, the Chair of the Police Federation for Northern Ireland, as his source for the belief that 'those who withhold their consent [from the RUC] range from disaffected drop-outs, to young people going through a rebellious phase to irreformable criminals and terrorists and those who support them'. Ibid., col. 64. Rodgers's comments are cited originally in 'Only rebels want RUC reforms, union told', *Irish News*, Belfast, 19 November 1997.
8 'Open and shut case: an inquiry should not weaken the RUC', *Times*, London, 29 April 1998.
9 'The RUC has a low intake from the minority community because people from that community fear they will be subject to the risk of death, mutilation or ostracism by the community in which they live if they join the RUC.' Robert McCartney, in *House of Commons Hansard Debates*, 15 December 1997, col. 75.
10 RUC, *A Fundamental Review of Policing: Summary and Key Findings* (Belfast: RUC, 1997), p. 9.
11 See Northern Ireland Affairs Committee, *Composition, Recruitment and Training of the RUC*, p. 31.
12 Ibid., p. 14. The Chief Constable referred to the figures in his

evidence to the committee, p. 31.
The *Times*, with one
enthusiastically partisan Scots
unionist among its leader writers,
exaggerated by some margin
when it claimed in an editorial
against RUC reform that the
proportion of Catholic applicants
had climbed to 'over 30 per cent
of the total' during this period.
Times, London, 28 April 1998.

13 'GAA cleric criticizes "failure on
rule 21" ', *Irish News*, Belfast,
8 June 1998. The argument is
highlighted by the RUC. See
Northern Ireland Affairs
Committee, *Composition,
Recruitment and Training of the RUC*,
p. 9.

14 John Brewer, 'The public and the
police,' in P. Stringer and G.
Robinson (eds.), *Social Attitudes in
Northern Ireland: The Second Report*
(Belfast: Blackstaff Press, 1992),
pp. 52–66.

15 Ibid., p. 62 and p. 65.

16 See 'Little to cheer about', *Irish
Independent*, Dublin, 21 March
1998, and 'There's so much to
lose', *Irish Independent*, 12 July
1998. More recently, O'Brien has
suggested that unionists should
consider negotiating a united
Ireland in order to keep the RUC,
Observer, London, 25 October
1998; see also Conor Cruise
O'Brien, *Memoir: My Life and
Times* (London: Profile Books,
1998), pp. 435ff. This is not an
argument for serious people and
merely shows the absurdities to
which intellectual extremism and
attention-seeking may lead.
O'Brien is the only public
intellectual of note in either part of
Ireland who opposes the Good
Friday Agreement.

17 Nigel Dodds, *RUC Reform* (Belfast:
DUP, 1996).

18 Sir Patrick Mayhew, the former
Conservative Secretary of State
for Northern Ireland, recently
called for nationalist politicians to

encourage Catholics to join the
RUC; see 'Mayhew says RUC could
be undermined by inquiry', *Irish
Times*, Dublin, 7 April 1998.

19 'Authority unveils policing
proposals', *Irish News*, Belfast,
26 March 1998.

20 'Open and shut case: an inquiry
should not weaken the RUC',
Times, London, 29 April 1998.

21 See Chapter 2.

22 *House of Commons Hansard Debates*,
15 December 1997, col. 49.

23 See A. Hamilton, L. Moore and
T. Trimble, *Policing a Divided
Society: Issues and Perceptions in
Northern Ireland* (Coleraine: Centre
for the Study of Conflict, 1995),
p. 13.

24 Andy Pollak (ed.), *A Citizens'
Inquiry: The Opsahl Report on
Northern Ireland* (Dublin: Lilliput
Press, 1993), p. 61.

25 Police Authority for Northern
Ireland, *Listening to the Community,
Working with the RUC* (Belfast:
PANI, 1998), p. 52.

26 John Brewer, Adrian Guelke, Ian
Hume, Edward Moxon-Browne
and Rick Wilford, *The Police,
Public Order and the State: Policing in
Great Britain, Northern Ireland, the
Irish Republic, the USA, Israel, South
Africa and China* (New York: St
Martin's Press, 1988), p. 49.

27 As already noted, the Catholic
share of applications dropped to
16 per cent in 1996.

28 The argument that surveys under-
report extreme views and over-
report moderate ones is widely
accepted – see John Whyte,
Interpreting Northern Ireland
(Oxford: Clarendon Press, 1990),
p. 84, and John McGarry and
Brendan O'Leary, *Explaining
Northern Ireland: Broken Images*
(Oxford: Basil Blackwell, 1995),
pp. 468–9, note 124. Note that
there may be an additional
problem with the Police
Authority's surveys. Graham
Ellison writes that 'the PANI data

has demonstrable under-representation of unskilled manual respondents. Among the Catholic community this group is the one most likely to have had negative or hostile encounters with the RUC and the group most likely to favour disbandment of the force given their political support for Sinn Féin. Similar patterns can be discerned in the NI Social Attitudes survey data where the proportion of Sinn Féin respondents is listed at 2.8 per cent (1992).' Northern Ireland Affairs Committee, *Composition, Recruitment and Training of the RUC*, p. 55.

29 Ronald Weitzer, *Policing under Fire: Ethnic Conflict and Police–Community Relations in Northern Ireland* (Albany: SUNY Press, 1995), p. 15. See also p. 312, note 13.

30 Also see ibid., Table 4.2, p. 86.

31 Catholics, in fact, were more likely to consider policing reform to be essential to a settlement (70 per cent) than the disbanding of all paramilitary groups (67 per cent). Colin Irwin, *The Search for a Settlement: The People's Choice* (Belfast: Fortnight Educational Trust, 1998), p. 3.

32 *Belfast Telegraph*, 18 May 1998.

33 These figures are taken from Police Authority for Northern Ireland, *Reflecting All Shades of Opinion* (Belfast: PANI, 1998), Table 11b. The October 1997 poll is the most flattering to the RUC of the three polls presented by the Police Authority. Earlier polls conducted in September 1996 and February 1997 offer a much bleaker picture of Catholic support. While 21 per cent of Catholics had a lot of confidence or total confidence in the police's public order role in the October 1997 survey, the figure for the two earlier surveys was 10 per cent. We have deliberately

highlighted the October poll, and used mostly polls presented by the Police Authority, to avoid the criticism that we are exaggerating the extent of Catholic opposition to the RUC. Ellison found from his own survey data that there was no appreciable strengthening of links between the RUC and Catholics in the year after the first IRA cease-fire. Northern Ireland Affairs Committee, *Composition, Recruitment and Training of the RUC*, pp. 263–4.

34 Dr Geoffrey Evans of Nuffield College has observed in a personal communication that 'the Northern Ireland Social Attitudes Survey data show weak differences between classes in their opinions of the RUC. Sometimes working-class respondents perceive more discrimination – amongst Catholics and Protestants – and sometimes the balance shifts to the middle class in both communities. However, there are problems with the measures of class, and their comparability over time. One cannot draw any very firm conclusions about class differences solely on these survey data.' (Note to B. O'L., 27 October 1998)

35 Whyte, *Interpreting Northern Ireland*, p. 88.

36 Cited in *Policing in a New Society*, p. 20.

37 As the Pat Finucane Centre for Human Rights observed in a submission to the Northern Ireland Affairs Committee of the House of Commons, if the RUC had 10 per cent Catholics in 1969, and 7.5 per cent in 1996, then republican intimidation can only have been responsible for, at most, reducing Catholic involvement by 2.5 per cent. Northern Ireland Affairs Committee, *Composition, Recruitment and Training of the RUC*, p. 454.

38 See Brendan O'Leary, 'The nature

of the Agreement' (the Ninth John Whyte Memorial Lecture), forthcoming in *Scottish Affairs* and *New Left Review*.

39 In the *Fortnight* poll of December 1997, taken before the Agreement, 70 per cent of Catholics thought that a complete reform of the police service was essential, but only 32 per cent thought 'reformed and shared government' was. The poll also showed that reform of policing was considered essential by more Catholics than was a British withdrawal (46 per cent). The relatively low support for the latter, however, may simply reflect the fact that it is unlikely to be realised in the near future. See Irwin, *Search for a Settlement*, p. 3.

2 Policing the enemy

1 Conor Brady, *Guardians of the Peace* (Dublin: Gill & Macmillan, 1974), p. 3. Brady's contrast needs one important qualification: London, where the largest and most dangerous 'mobs' caused anxieties among the governing class, was policed by a metropolitan force that was under direct ministerial supervision – though it was unarmed.

2 For a more complete and nuanced discussion of the partition of Ireland see John McGarry and Brendan O'Leary, *Explaining Northern Ireland: Broken Images* (Oxford: Basil Blackwell, 1995), Chapter 1.

3 In 1924 the ratio of police to population was 1:160 in Northern Ireland, 1:669 in England and Wales, and 1:751 in Scotland. See Ronald Weitzer, *Policing under Fire: Ethnic Conflict and Police–Community Relations in Northern Ireland* (Albany: SUNY Press, 1995), p. 34.

4 Section 1, subsection 1 of the Civil Authorities (Special Powers) Act (1922): 'The Civil Authority shall have power, in respect of persons, matters and things within the jurisdiction of the Government of Northern Ireland to take all such steps and issue all such orders as may be necessary for preserving the peace and maintaining order.' Section 1, subsection 3: 'If any person does any act of such a nature as to be calculated to be prejudicial to the preservation of the peace or the maintenance of order in Northern Ireland and not specifically provided for in the regulations, he shall be deemed to be guilty of an offence against the regulations.'

5 Weitzer, *Policing under Fire*, p. 32.

6 Roland Moyle, interview with Brendan O'Leary, 3 January 1991. Merlyn Rees, the Secretary of State for Northern Ireland from 1974 to 1976, similarly recalled: 'The stories one heard about the RUC inspectors. When one visited Fermanagh to see the Prime Minister Brooke, he had to go through the side door like a servant.' Interview with Brendan O'Leary, 18 December 1990. Weitzer reports a statement by the Minister of Home Affairs during sectarian disturbances in 1935, in which he apparently warned constables that they would be punished if they acted too zealously against Protestants, *Policing under Fire*, p. 47.

7 An unintentionally risible *apologia* for the B Specials can be found in Sir Arthur Hezlet, *The 'B' Specials: A History of the Ulster Special Constabulary* (London: Pan Books, 1973).

8 Weitzer, *Policing under Fire*, p. 39.

9 The committee on the reorganisation of the police was formed in early 1922. It recommended that one third of the new force should be drawn from Catholic members of the RIC

and from the population at large, and two thirds from Protestants in the RIC and the USC. Weitzer thinks that the one-third quota was in fact designed to put a limit on Catholic numbers eligible for recruitment, given that well over half the RIC's members in Belfast, and over 80 per cent throughout Ireland, had been Catholics. Part of the explanation may also have been financial. The UK government had made generous pension arrangements for RIC members, and had stipulated that Belfast and Dublin should pay for these. See John Brewer, Adrian Guelke, Ian Hume, Edward Moxon-Browne and Rick Wilford, *The Police, Public Order and the State: Policing in Great Britain, Northern Ireland, the Irish Republic, the USA, Israel, South Africa and China* (New York: St Martin's Press, 1988), p. 49. Whatever the sources of the committee's apparently generous response towards Catholic recruitment, it needs to be recalled that Catholics in the RIC were, almost by definition, unrepresentative of Catholic and nationalist political opinion.

10   Michael Farrell, *Arming the Protestants* (London: Pluto Press, 1983), p. 267.

11   See the discussion above in Chapter 1, pp. 14–22.

12   Weitzer, *Policing under Fire*, p. 39.

13   Brewer *et al.*, *The Police, Public Order and the State*, p. 50.

14   See Brendan O'Leary and John McGarry, *The Politics of Antagonism: Understanding Northern Ireland* (London: Athlone Press, 1996, 2nd edition), Chapter 3.

15   Gerry Hogan and Clive Walker, *Political Violence and the Law in Ireland* (Manchester: Manchester University Press, 1989), p. 14.

16   *Disturbances in Northern Ireland: Report of the Commission Appointed by the Governor of Northern Ireland* (the Cameron Report) (Belfast: HMSO, 1969); *Violence and Civil Disturbances in Northern Ireland in 1969* (the Scarman Report) (Belfast: HMSO, 1972).

17   Weitzer, *Policing under Fire*, p. 61.

18   Weitzer, *Policing under Fire*; John Brewer with Kathleen Magee, *Inside the RUC: Routine Policing in a Divided Society* (Oxford: Clarendon Press, 1991).

19   *Irish News*, Belfast, 21 February 1998. While these figures underline increased professionalism, they are also partly a reflection of a key weakness with the RUC. The disproportionate success rates against loyalists result partly from the greater intelligence that comes in from loyalist communities, which confirms that the police have greater support there than they have within republican-dominated communities.

20   This is the position of the larger and more moderate of Northern Ireland's two main nationalist political parties, the SDLP: 'The policing and political problems of Northern Ireland are intertwined and interlocked; we cannot solve one without the other; if we fail to solve one, the other is incapable of resolution.' SDLP, *Policing in Northern Ireland* (Belfast: SDLP, 1995), p. 1.

21   O'Leary and McGarry, *The Politics of Antagonism*, p. 197.

22   Ibid., p. 25.

23   Weitzer, *Policing under Fire*, p. 64.

24   Hogan and Walker, *Political Violence*, p. 27. For constructive proposals on how to reform emergency legislation, see the work of Conor Gearty and John Kimbell, *Terrorism and the Rule of Law: A Report on the Laws Relating to Political Violence in Great Britain and Northern Ireland* (London: Civil Liberties Research Unit, School of Law, King's College, 1995).

25   Figures from Kevin Boyle and

Tom Hadden, *Northern Ireland: The Choice* (Harmondsworth: Penguin, 1994), p. 86.

26 Peter Taylor, *Beating the Terrorists?* (Harmondsworth: Penguin, 1980).

27 Amnesty International, *Report of an Amnesty International Mission to Northern Ireland* (New York: Amnesty International, 1978); *Report of the Committee of Inquiry into Police Interrogation Procedures in Northern Ireland* (the Bennett Report) (London: HMSO, 1979).

28 S. Greer, 'Supergrasses and the legal system in Britain and Northern Ireland', *Law Quarterly Review*, 102 (1986): pp. 198–249.

29 John Stalker, *Stalker* (Harmondsworth: Penguin, 1988).

30 Dermot Walsh, 'The Royal Ulster Constabulary: a law unto themselves?', in M. Tomlinson, T. Varley and C. McCullough (eds.), *Whose Law and Order?* (Belfast: Sociological Association of Ireland, 1988).

31 See Conor Cruise O'Brien's arguments in Chapter 1, pp. 11–12, and note 16.

3 Who should be in the police?

1 Anarchists might insist on a prior 'why' question: 'Why have a police at all?' They think that that government is good which governs least, and hence that no government is best of all. Our answer to anarchists is modernist, statist and realist. Ireland and Britain are post-tribal and post-agrarian. Modernist and statist peoples just do not and should not leave policing to the doubtful and arbitrary merits of self-help and feuding. They rightly treat policing services, or their functional equivalents, as necessary instruments for protecting people and their rights, including their personal security and property rights. This is, of course, compatible with considerable variation in the nature and accountability of policing services. The anarchist's only feasible alternative to policing is a regime in which everybody acts as their own paramilitary, or hires others for 'protection', a regime that we suspect most Northern Irish people would reject.

2 While Catholics comprise 7.5 per cent of the overall RUC, they represent 8.2 per cent of 'regular' RUC officers, 6.9 per cent of the full-time Reserve, and 4.8 per cent of the part-time Reserve. See Northern Ireland Affairs Committee, *Composition, Recruitment and Training of the RUC*, Vol. II, *Minutes of Evidence and Appendices* (London: Stationery Office, 1998), p. 14. Some sections of the regular RUC have slightly higher proportions of Protestants, while others have lower: both the Special Branch and Urban Mobile Support Units, which have attracted particular criticism from nationalists, have lower proportions of Catholics (6.4 and 5.9 per cent respectively) than the overall force. (We have rounded all numbers to one decimal point – J. McG. and B. O'L.)

3 See John Brewer, Adrian Guelke, Ian Hume, Edward Moxon-Browne and Rick Wilford, *The Police, Public Order and the State: Policing in Great Britain, Northern Ireland, the Irish Republic, the USA, Israel, South Africa and China* (New York: St Martin's Press, 1988), p. 112.

4 The ethnographic study of Brewer and Magee found that Catholic officers, in an effort to fit into the RUC, displayed attitudes similar to the dominant Protestant/unionist culture within the force. They say that some of

the most blatantly anti-Catholic remarks they heard were uttered by Catholic policemen. John Brewer with Kathleen Magee, *Inside the RUC: Routine Policing in a Divided Society* (Oxford: Clarendon Press, 1991), p. 250. A study of part-time members of the RUC produced similar findings; see R. Mapstone, 'The attitudes of police in a divided society', *British Journal of Criminology*, 32, 2 (1992): pp. 183–92.

5 Graham Ellison makes the claim in a memorandum to the Northern Ireland Affairs Committee. See *Composition, Recruitment and Training of the RUC*, p. 267. Ellison does not produce figures, but acknowledges that the numbers of non-Northern Irish Catholics are likely to be small. Vigorous advertising and recruitment among Catholics in the Republic of Ireland could, of course, change that.

6 Ibid., p. 37.

7 Ibid., p. 15.

8 In 1969, the RUC had 3,044 members. See John Brewer *et al.*, *The Police, Public Order and the State*, p. 56.

9 The lower range is from Paul Bew, Henry Patterson and Paul Teague, *Northern Ireland: Between War and Peace* (London: Lawrence and Wishart, 1997), p. 102. The higher range is from the Committee for the Administration of Justice, *A Submission from the Committee for the Administration of Justice (CAJ) to the Police Authority (PANI) Consultation on the Future of Policing in Northern Ireland* (Belfast: CAJ, August 1995), p. 17.

10 In evidence to the Northern Ireland Affairs Committee, the Chief Constable suggested that the figure would have to be 'something in the order of less than 8,000 officers overall'. Northern Ireland Affairs Committee, *Composition, Recruitment and Training of the RUC*, p. 29. The Police Authority reports the Chief Constable and Her Majesty's Inspector of Constabulary opting for 'around 6,000–7,000 officers'. Police Authority for Northern Ireland, *Listening to the Community, Working with the RUC* (Belfast: PANI, 1998), p. 52.

11 The temporary transfer of police from English and Scottish services is not an insuperable problem, and the British government could address this problem, in a new era of North–South co-operation, by allowing the police in Northern Ireland to call for assistance from the Garda Síochána, a police service with which, in the Chief Constable's view, the RUC enjoys excellent relations (Northern Ireland Affairs Committee, *Composition, Recruitment and Training of the RUC*, p. 41). Such a policy would meet the terms of reference of the Patten Commission (see Appendix A to this book, pp. 115–19).

12 Bob Cooper of the Fair Employment Commission (FEC) also favours a larger force than could be justified for law-and-order needs, on the basis that it would provide more jobs for Catholics. 'RUC needs more Catholics says FEC', *Irish News*, Belfast, 26 March 1998. The FEC argues that a fixed proportion of police jobs should go to Catholics and that the law should be changed to permit this target. Northern Ireland Affairs Committee, *Composition, Recruitment and Training of the RUC*, p. 282. By contrast Ivan Topping, a law lecturer at the University of Ulster, argues that it would be easier to obtain a representative police if its numbers were small – presumably because the smaller the total of police the easier it

would be to recruit a proportionate number of nationalists. This is true but neglects the interests of serving officers. Ibid., p. 240.

13   PANI, *Listening to the Community*, p. 60.

14   Workers' Party spokesperson Paddy Lynn maintains, 'People have to stop thinking on the lines of Catholics or Protestants in the police but start thinking along the lines of a service based not on religious quotas but on merit. While there is recognition that there has to be changes within the structures of the RUC, religious head counts are not the answer. What we want, and what the people of Northern Ireland need, is a police service that is accountable, impartial, independent, effective, responsive, professional, unarmed and civilianised.' 'Authority unveils policing proposals', *Irish News*, Belfast, 26 March 1998.

15   PANI, *Listening to the Community*, p. 63.

16   A recent *Times* editorial claimed that 'after the IRA called its cease-fire the proportion of applicants from the Catholic community for jobs with the RUC rose to over 30 per cent of the total, strikingly close to the sectarian balance in the Province'. 'An open and shut case', *Times*, London, 29 April 1998. This is unimpressive reporting, and suggests editorialising with factual insecurity: (1) the figures referred to applicants and not successful recruits, and Catholics are more likely to be the former than the latter; (2) the actual proportionate increase in applications was to 20 per cent, not 30 per cent, an error of magnitude of 50 per cent; and (3) 30 per cent is not 'strikingly close' to the religious balance – cultural Catholics represent over 43 per cent of the population,

which is a considerable distance from 30, never mind 20 per cent.

17   Northern Ireland Affairs Committee, *Composition, Recruitment and Training of the RUC*, p. 30.

18   PANI, *Listening to the Community*, p. 63.

19   Apart from deflating the 'green card' myth, these figures throw into question the RUC's claim that an applicant's religion 'will have no bearing on whether [s/he is] successful during our selection procedures'. Northern Ireland Affairs Committee, *Composition, Recruitment and Training of the RUC*, p. 15.

20   In 1995, often cited as a banner year because of the increase in the Catholic application rate to 20 per cent, 44 Catholic officers were recruited into a force of 12,819. Ibid., p. 14.

21   Our figures are based on the RUC's current full-time complement of 11,412 police officers. We have assumed that serving Catholic officers will retire or be made redundant at the same rate as Protestant officers. Reducing overall police numbers from 11,412 to 5,000, therefore, would reduce the number of serving Catholic officers from 900 to 394.

22   Women constitute just over 10 per cent of the current police, and are disproportionately concentrated in the lower ranks: 17 per cent of constables, 4 per cent of inspectors, and 2.5 per cent of superintendents are female. See Mary O'Rawe and Linda Moore, *Human Rights on Duty: Principles for Better Policing – International Lessons for Northern Ireland* (Belfast: CAJ, 1997), pp. 24–6. Increased numbers of females in the police service might help change its image and internal culture, making it seem less threatening to all, not just nationalists.

23   Trevor Jones and Tim Newburn,

'Policing and disaffected communities', in Standing Advisory Commission on Human Rights, *Report for 1995–1996* (London: HMSO, 1996), pp. 257–8; Ronald Weitzer, *Policing under Fire: Ethnic Conflict and Police–Community Relations in Northern Ireland* (Albany: SUNY Press, 1995), pp. 109–10.

24 Different assumptions will produce different results. Bew, Patterson and Teague have proposed a two-stage model which would reduce the size of the RUC from 11,500 (full-time) to 4,000–4,500 and make it representative of the population within seven years. In the first stage, which would take three years, they propose downsizing the RUC by 4,600 through eliminating the Reserve (3,100) and by 'natural wastage' (1,500). The three advocate a simultaneous 'massive campaign to recruit Catholics', with the objective being to recruit 1,000 Catholics. In the second, four-year stage, the RUC would be downsized by a further 4,000. At the end of the period, the RUC would be operating at its minimum efficient scale of 4,000–4,500 and would be broadly representative of the population. See Bew *et al.*, *Northern Ireland: Between War and Peace*, p. 102. Their suggestions involve more job losses for Protestants and fewer job gains for Catholics than ours do – nor do Bew, Patterson and Teague explain why a 'massive campaign to recruit Catholics' into the RUC would succeed. We do not think that Catholics will join the police unless policing undergoes a number of necessary major changes, especially in national impartiality, that Bew, Patterson and Teague do not address.

25 This is based on the RUC's figure that roughly 200 vacancies occur each year. 2,166 officers have served for more than twenty years. See Northern Ireland Affairs Committee, *Composition, Recruitment and Training of the RUC*, p. 18.

26 Michael Brogden, 'An agenda for post-Troubles policing in Northern Ireland: the South African precedent', *Liverpool Law Review*, XVII (I), 1995, p. 25.

27 See the Discussion Paper, *Principles for Policing in Northern Ireland* (Belfast: Stationery Office, 1998), p. 5.

28 Short Brothers of Belfast has recently won a court case against the conventional union practice of 'last in, first out'. There is a widespread view that younger RUC officers are more enlightened than their senior counterparts, which, if true, would suggest that redundancies should be based on a 'first in, first out' principle. This, as far as we know, has not been tested. Survey data do not suggest that among the general public the young are more enlightened in their attitudes than their elders. Anecdotal evidence also throws some doubt on the theory. Recently, an RUC trainee told a non-RUC instructor who was lecturing about human rights that the RUC would have solved 'the problem' a long time ago if it had not been for his sort. Another recruit told the lecturer that he 'had no idea what it was like out there for an RUC officer' – without explaining how he himself knew – interview with a Queen's University lecturer, March 1998. One study describes younger police as being more aggressive than older mature officers; see A. Hamilton, L. Moore and T. Trimble, *Policing a Divided Society: Issues and Perceptions in Northern Ireland* (Coleraine: Centre for the Study of Conflict, 1995), p. 102.

29 See Brogden, 'An agenda for

post–Troubles policing', p. 25. Michael Brogden also suggests that RUC officers, who have gathered considerable skills in fighting subversives, should be able to find high-paying jobs in several other countries. As we are sure he would agree, however, the use of such expertise in any country would have to be carefully controlled.

30 The figures are for 1997/8. See PANI, *Listening to the Community*, p. 59.

31 Brewer *et al.*, *The Police, Public Order and the State*, pp. 48–9. James Craig and Michael Collins also signed a pact that provided for the B Specials in Belfast to be half Catholic and half Protestant, although this did not materialise. Weitzer, *Policing under Fire*, p. 41.

32 The last benefit has led Bob Cooper, Chair of the Fair Employment Commission, to call for more Catholics in the RUC. 'RUC needs more Catholics says FEC', *Irish News*, Belfast, 26 March 1998.

33 Secretary of State Dr Mowlam wrote recently that 'officers must continue to be recruited, appointed and promoted openly and fairly, in accordance with recognised standards of practice, based upon merit'. *Belfast Telegraph*, 1 May 1998.

34 Northern Ireland Affairs Committee, *Composition, Recruitment and Training of the RUC*, p. 31.

35 Between 1 January 1994 and 20 February 1998, police arrested 2,372 loyalists compared to 1,463 republicans; and 42 loyalists and 24 republicans were charged with murder, *Irish News*, Belfast, 21 February 1998. This discrepancy is partly explained by the greater willingness of loyalist communities to give information to the RUC, and by the greater familiarity of the police with loyalist areas. It may also be the case, of course, that loyalists were involved in more offences during this period, and/or that they were less efficient or secretive than republican paramilitaries.

36 Michael Farrell, *Arming the Protestants* (London: Pluto Press, 1983), p. 189.

37 In the United States, for example, one of the central arguments both for quotas in public institutions and for the redistricting of electoral constituencies is that black constituents feel more comfortable, and are more likely to voice their concerns, if their representatives (and the agents of government) are black. See Jane Mansbridge, 'A descriptive representation in communicative settings of distrust, uncrystallized interests, and historically denigrated status', paper presented to a conference on Citizenship in Diverse Societies, Toronto, Ontario, 4–5 October 1997, pp. 21–4.

38 In the early 1990s, Bishop Edward Daly of Derry complained that, to the best of his knowledge, there was not 'a single police officer living on the west bank of the Foyle. It's a community of 80,000 people and not a single police officer living in that area.' Cited in Hamilton *et al.*, *Policing a Divided Society*, pp. 48–9.

39 John Edwards, *Affirmative Action in a Sectarian Society: Fair Employment Policy in Northern Ireland* (Aldershot: Avebury, 1995), p. 15.

40 PUP, *Submission to the Northern Ireland Office by the Progressive Unionist Party on Policing and Related Matters* (Belfast: PUP, 1995), p. 2.

41 In the DUP's view, this is evidence of a 'green card', that is, unfair promotion. As Ian Paisley puts it, 'Roman Catholics in the police force have the best possible time.

They move to the top posts because of their religion.' *House of Commons Hansard Debates*, 15 December 1997, col. 83. (See also the comments by DUP deputy leader Peter Robinson, in Northern Ireland Affairs Committee, *Composition, Recruitment and Training of the RUC*, p. 35.) Given that Catholics constitute a smaller proportion of the police now (7.5 per cent) than they did in 1969 (10 per cent), it may be that Catholics are proportionally more senior than Protestants. More important, HM Inspector of Constabulary, Colin Smith, found that 30 per cent of Catholics who applied for promotion to sergeant were successful, compared with 28 per cent of Protestants – hardly definitive evidence for Dr Paisley's beliefs. Since he also found that Catholics are considerably less likely to apply for promotion, the DUP's case collapses. 'Inspectorate reveals lack of Catholic applications', *Irish News*, Belfast, 9 February 1998.

42 The Imperial Grand Chapter of the British Commonwealth, in a memorandum submitted to the House of Commons, wrongly claims that the 'higher ranks' of the RUC are 'about 40 per cent Catholic'. Northern Ireland Affairs Committee, *Composition, Recruitment and Training of the RUC*, p. 277.

43 See O'Rawe and Moore, *Human Rights on Duty*, p. 245.

44 See ibid., p. 144; Brogden, 'An agenda for post-Troubles policing', p. 10; Kevin Boyle and Tom Hadden, *Northern Ireland: The Choice* (Harmondsworth: Penguin, 1994), p. 202; Colm Campbell, *Policing in a New Society* (Belfast: Centre for Research and Documentation, 1994), p. 8.

4 Towards a nationally impartial police

1 Padraig O'Malley, 'Northern Ireland's identity gulf can't be overcome by police reform', *Boston Globe*, 19 May 1998.

2 Nationalists' preferred partisan designations are 'the North of Ireland' or 'the Six Counties', terms that do not recognise partition.

3 The Police Authority for Northern Ireland (PANI) and the Chief Constable have recognised that it is not the job of the police to defend the Union. Northern Ireland Affairs Committee, *Composition, Recruitment and Training of the RUC*, Vol. II, *Minutes of Evidence and Appendices* (London: Stationery Office, 1998), p. 60. Nevertheless PANI deliberately tries to give the impression that most people are happy with the RUC's name and symbols: its Chief Executive has declared, 'I think we need to be clear about this, that the bulk of those responding [to PANI's surveys] volunteered that they wished no change whatsoever to either the name of the RUC or to its uniform or to anything associated with it.' Ibid., p. 61. When an organisation has a chief executive who cannot interpret palpable evidence before his own eyes, its days are numbered.

4 Following a recent report by the Northern Ireland Affairs Committee suggesting that the flag be no longer displayed on the Twelfth of July, the Chief Constable discontinued the practice. 'RUC won't fly flag on parade day', *Daily Telegraph*, London, 28 July 1998. The flag continues to be flown on other public holidays.

5 See Ardoyne Association, *Neighbourhood Police Service*

(Belfast: Ardoyne Association, circa 1995), p. 19.

6 'New RUC management structures proposed', *Irish Times*, Dublin, 2 May 1996.

7 Flanagan told the committee, 'research is that it is not the sort of issue that some people make it and therefore I come to the conclusion that it would not help me in the significant way that people would suggest in terms of attracting many more recruits of the Catholic faith'. Northern Ireland Affairs Committee, *Composition, Recruitment and Training of the RUC*, p. 42.

8 The Chief Constable maintains, 'Certainly there are, in the dining rooms of the Royal Ulster Constabulary, portraits of Her Majesty. I do not think those can, in any terms, be construed as offensive. I do not think that can, in any terms, be construed as offending against a neutral working environment. . . . [T]he flying of the Union flag itself I cannot see as being offensive; I cannot see as being at odds with the provision of a neutral working environment.' Ibid., p. 33.

9 *House of Commons Hansard Debates*, 15 December 1997, col. 74. McCartney states, 'There is no question of someone in Surrey or in Kent being emptied out of the United Kingdom. Therefore symbols in those areas perhaps do not matter so much. . . . Now consider a situation in which one feels that one's identity and citizenship are constantly under threat. . . . Suddenly, symbols of one's identity – the Crown, the Queen and the royal appellation of the Royal Ulster Constabulary – become important.'

10 Police Authority for Northern Ireland, *Listening to the Community, Working with the RUC* (Belfast: PANI, 1998), p. 53.

11 Andy Pollak (ed.), *A Citizens'*

Inquiry: The Opsahl Report on Northern Ireland (Dublin: Lilliput Press, 1993), p. 62.

12 Colin Irwin, *The Search for a Settlement: The People's Choice* (Belfast: Fortnight Educational Trust, 1998), p. 9. There is some controversy about how strongly Catholics wish to change the RUC's name. An earlier poll, conducted in 1995, indicated that 49 per cent of Catholics wanted a name change (Police Authority for Northern Ireland, *Everyone's Police: A Partnership for Change* [Belfast: PANI, 1996], Appendix 6, Table 6). Given the widespread agreement that opinion polls exaggerate moderation (see Chapter 1 above, note 28), we believe that even this survey, often cited by the Chief Constable, suggests that the name of the RUC is a significant problem for Catholics. However, doubtless the Patten Commission is doing its own polling on this. If and when it does, might we suggest the following question, which provides a reasonable alternative, one that is consistent with recent legislative change, namely, 'Are you in favour of renaming the RUC as the Northern Ireland Police Service?'

13 Irwin, *Search for a Settlement*, p. 9.

14 PANI, *Listening to the Community*, p. 53. The report points out that opinion in Northern Ireland is 'sharply divided' on this issue.

15 Our sincere thanks go to Dr Diarmuid Ó Mathúna of the Dublin Institute for Advanced Studies, for his careful advice on the Gaelic language in these matters.

16 The Committee for the Administration of Justice (CAJ) has recommended changes broadly along these lines, as have academic commentators, as well as former members of the Police Authority. The CAJ calls for the

RUC's name to be changed to Northern Ireland Police Service and rejects as 'fudge' the changes in the 1998 Police (NI) Act. See CAJ, *A Submission from the Committee for the Administration of Justice (CAJ) on the Police (NI) Bill* (Belfast: CAJ, February 1998), p. 3. A. Hamilton, L. Moore and T. Trimble argue that a change to the name and symbols 'strongly linking the force to a state from which they have felt alienated, would seem to be essential elements in making the police more acceptable to Catholics'. See *Policing a Divided Society: Issues and Perceptions in Northern Ireland* (Coleraine: Centre for the Study of Conflict, 1995), p. 13. The former Chair of the Police Authority, David Cook, has called for there to be introduced 'without delay a balanced accommodation in regard to symbols'. See 'Preparing the RUC for historic changes', *Irish News*, Belfast, 5 February 1998.

17 One former member of the Police Authority, Chris Ryder, has argued that there is 'compelling evidence' that the RUC is in breach of fair employment legislation because of its failure to maintain a neutral working environment. See Roger MacGinty, 'Policing and the Northern Ireland peace process', *Cain Web Service* (Coleraine: Centre for the Study of Conflict, 1997), p. 3.

18 John Brewer with Kathleen Magee, *Inside the RUC: Routine Policing in a Divided Society* (Oxford: Clarendon Press, 1991), pp. 247, 250.

19 R. Mapstone, 'The attitudes of police in a divided society', *British Journal of Criminology*, 32, 2 (1992): pp. 183–92.

20 Graham Ellison, 'Professionalism in the Royal Ulster Constabulary: An Examination of the Institutional Discourse'

(unpublished PhD, University of Ulster, 1997).

21 Chris Ryder, 'A chance to re-root policing culture in the North', *Irish Times*, Dublin, 8 January 1998.

22 *Sunday Business Post*, Dublin, 15 March 1998.

23 When asked to give their reasons for not joining the police, 22 per cent of Catholics said they thought they would be 'badly treated' (see Table 1.1, p. 10). The RUC's own internal research suggests that this belief is more than a mere perception.

24 PANI, *Listening to the Community*, p. 70.

25 Northern Ireland Affairs Committee, *Composition, Recruitment and Training of the RUC*, p. 38.

26 PANI, *Listening to the Community*, p. 70.

27 Trevor Jones and Tim Newburn, 'Policing and disaffected communities', in Standing Advisory Commission on Human Rights, *Report for 1995–1996* (London: HMSO, 1996), p. 261. They argue (p. 266) that the recruitment of minorities (and women) is 'likely to impact in positive ways both on the internal police culture and on relations between the service and those who are policed'.

28 'Orange Order' in D. J. Hickey and J. E. Doherty (eds.), *A Dictionary of Irish History 1800–1980* (Dublin: Gill & Macmillan, 1980), pp. 449–50.

29 Aoghan Mulcahy's research is published as one of the appendices in Northern Ireland Affairs Committee, *Composition, Recruitment and Training of the RUC*, p. 249. His figure is based on the fact that the Orange Order acknowledges 39 of the officers killed since 1969 as having been its members, suggesting that 13 per cent of police casualties were

Orangemen. It may be that today fewer members of the RUC join the Orange Order but we have no way of knowing. A simple extrapolation from 13 per cent of the current total of RUC members would suggest a figure in the region of 1,670 Orange Order members, but it may well be that RUC officers belong to other secret or loyal orders.

30 Northern Ireland Affairs Committee, *Composition, Recruitment and Training of the RUC*, p. 34.

31 Irwin, *Search for a Settlement*, p. 9.

32 'Federation chief is slammed. Anger over Orange Order comments', *Irish News*, Belfast, 12 May 1997.

33 'RUC wants officers to leave the lodges', *Daily Telegraph*, London, 14 January 1998.

34 'RUC under fire', *Irish News*, Belfast, 5 February 1998.

35 PANI, *Listening to the Community*, p. 54.

36 'The Authority has *no reason* to doubt the integrity and impartiality of the RUC and has consistently defended its record over many years but it does consider that a register of interests would strengthen in the public mind the independence and impartiality of the police'. Ibid. (emphasis ours), p. 54.

37 Northern Ireland Affairs Committee, *Composition, Recruitment and Training of the RUC*, Vol. I, *Report and Proceedings of the Committee* (London: Stationery Office, 1998), para. 51.

38 For comments along these lines, see the Alliance Party's paper, *Police Authority Consultation Process* (Belfast: APNI, May 1995).

39 Even though the last attempt to disarm and demilitarise the police (following the Hunt Report) took place during escalating violence, it attracted, according to Weitzer, 'a remarkable degree of support': one 1970 poll found a slight majority of police officers in favour of disarming. See Ronald Weitzer, *Policing under Fire: Ethnic Conflict and Police–Community Relations in Northern Ireland* (Albany: SUNY Press, 1995), p. 66.

40 Armed units of the British police include the Diplomatic and Royal Protection Group; some Special Branch officers; members of the Anti-Terrorist and Robbery squads; and officers at Heathrow airport. John Brewer, Adrian Guelke, Ian Hume, Edward Moxon-Browne and Rick Wilford, *The Police, Public Order and the State: Policing in Great Britain, Northern Ireland, the Irish Republic, the USA, Israel, South Africa and China* (New York: St Martin's Press, 1988), pp. 23–4.

41 One of the RUC's problems is that, because it is a unitary organisation, the whole force has been identified with the excesses of a few officers.

42 *Observer*, London, 23 August 1998.

43 Mary O'Rawe and Linda Moore, *Human Rights on Duty: Principles for Better Policing – International Lessons for Northern Ireland* (Belfast: CAJ, 1997), pp. 107–8.

44 65 per cent of Protestants thought that a 'Bill of Rights that guarantees equality for all' was either 'essential' (37 per cent) or 'desirable' (28 per cent). Support was even greater among Catholics: 91 per cent of them thought such a bill was either essential (78 per cent) or desirable (13 per cent). Protestants, however, also put great importance on 'security' questions and may not be as supportive of a bill that restrains the security forces. Figures from Irwin, *Search for a Settlement*, p. 5.

45 Christopher McCrudden, John McGarry and Brendan O'Leary, 'Equality and social justice',

Sunday Business Post, Dublin, 10
May 1998, and Brendan O'Leary,
'The nature of the Agreement'
(the Ninth John Whyte Memorial
Lecture), forthcoming in *Scottish
Affairs* and *New Left Review*.

5 Decentralising policing

1 Royal Ulster Constabulary, *A
Fundamental Review of Policing:
Summary and Key Findings* (Belfast:
RUC, 1997), pp. 6–7.
2 It does not mean what Conor
Cruise O'Brien, the only Irish
public intellectual of note, North
or South, who opposes the
Agreement, suggests by
'community policing', namely,
'A sweet sounding name for the
scrapping of the RUC and its
replacement by a system in which
each set of paramilitaries would
have full control instead of only
partial control, as at present, of its
own turf.' See 'I regret only one
thing', *Irish Independent*, Dublin,
31 October 1998.
3 The differences between the status
quo and a two-tier policing
structure may be obvious to most
of us, but there appears to be some
(deliberate?) confusion over what
'two-tier' policing means. The
Chief Constable has argued that
the RUC currently provides a
'service in tiers'. 'Authority
unveils policing proposals',
Irish News, Belfast, 26 March
1998.
4 This point is also made by A.
Hamilton, L. Moore and T.
Trimble, *Policing a Divided Society:
Issues and Perceptions in Northern
Ireland* (Coleraine: Centre for the
Study of Conflict, 1995), p. 14.
5 Colm Campbell, 'Policing in
Ireland: the historical balance
sheet', in *Policing in a New Society*
(Belfast: Centre for Research and
Documentation, 1994), p. 5.

6 R. Mawby, *Comparative Policing
Issues: The British and American
Experience in International
Perspective* (London: Unwin
Hyman, 1990), p. 85.
7 Mary O'Rawe and Linda Moore,
*Human Rights on Duty: Principles for
Better Policing – International Lessons
for Northern Ireland* (Belfast: CAJ,
1997), pp. 185 and 191.
8 Fr R. Murray, 'Hunt for an
alternative', *Fortnight*, 316, April
1993, pp. 32–3; Brian Lennon SJ,
*After the Cease-fires: Catholics and the
Future of Northern Ireland* (Dublin:
Columba Press, 1995), p. 153; Dr
M. Hayes in Northern Ireland
Affairs Committee, *Composition,
Recruitment and Training of the RUC*,
Vol. II, *Minutes of Evidence and
Appendices* (London: Stationery
Office, 1998), p. 65; Michael
Brogden, *Two-tiered Policing: A
Middle Way for Northern Ireland?*
(Belfast: Democratic Dialogue,
1998); SDLP, *Policing in
Northern Ireland* (Belfast: SDLP,
1995), p. 9.
9 In these cases, the officers
employed by the local police
normally transfer to the
provincial police, or vice versa.
10 SDLP, *Policing in Northern Ireland*,
p. 9.
11 Andy Pollak (ed.), *A Citizens'
Inquiry: The Opsahl Report on
Northern Ireland* (Dublin: Lilliput
Press, 1993), pp. 277–9.
12 Sinn Féin, *Policing in Transition: A
Legacy of Repression, an Opportunity
for Justice* (Belfast: Sinn Féin,
1996), p. 12.
13 Colin Irwin, *The Search for a
Settlement: The People's Choice*
(Belfast: Fortnight Educational
Trust, 1998), p. 10.
14 See *House of Commons Hansard
Debates*, 15 December 1997, cols.
63 and 76.
15 Northern Ireland Affairs
Committee, *Composition,
Recruitment and Training of the RUC*,
p. 36.

16 'It would lead to insuperable problems of consistency and coordination, administrative overlap and waste, as well as operational confusion . . . it is impractical.' Evidence by Chris Ryder to the Northern Ireland Affairs Committee, *Composition, Recruitment and Training of the RUC*, p. 271. This reasoning would imply that Canadian and Swiss policing should long ago have ground to a halt in an expensive catastrophe. Travelling abroad is good for specialists in Northern Irish public policy.

17 Ibid., p. 37.

18 O'Rawe and Moore, *Human Rights on Duty*, p. 191.

19 John Brewer, Adrian Guelke, Ian Hume, Edward Moxon-Browne and Rick Wilford, *The Police, Public Order and the State: Policing in Great Britain, Northern Ireland, the Irish Republic, the USA, Israel, South Africa and China* (New York: St Martin's Press, 1988), p. 15.

20 See Michael Brogden, 'Reforming the Royal Ulster Constabulary – a two-tiered police service for Northern Ireland', in Northern Ireland Affairs Committee, *Composition, Recruitment and Training of the RUC*, pp. 284–94.

21 *House of Commons Hansard Debates*, 15 December 1997, cols. 63 and 76.

22 This restriction should apply equally to army personnel found guilty of murder by the courts. According to reliable Labour Party sources, Secretary of State for Northern Ireland, Dr Mo Mowlam, expressed her agreement with this position in October 1998. Given that Secretary of State for Defence, George Robertson, has allowed convicted army personnel to be reinstated, he would appear not to agree.

23 Kevin Boyle and Tom Hadden argue that a separate or supplemental police service in nationalist areas 'would help to diminish the influence of paramilitaries'. Boyle and Hadden, *Northern Ireland: The Choice* (Harmondsworth: Penguin, 1994), p. 8.

24 Ronald Weitzer, *Policing under Fire: Ethnic Conflict and Police–Community Relations in Northern Ireland* (Albany: SUNY Press, 1995), pp. 28–9. The police force had 160 members, of whom between five and seven were Catholic.

25 The 1864 commission that looked into abuses by the local Belfast force considered its overwhelmingly one-sided composition to be at the heart of the problem. Ibid., p. 29.

26 O'Rawe and Moore, *Human Rights on Duty*, p. 187.

27 The first two of these concerns are raised by the Alliance Party in its argument for retaining a single policing service in Northern Ireland. See Alliance Party, *Police Authority Consultation Process* (Belfast: APNI, May 1995), p. 5.

28 O'Rawe and Moore, *Human Rights on Duty*, p. 185.

29 Graphical illustrations of our proposals can be found in figures 6.1 and 6.2, on pp. 107 and 108.

6 Creating a democratically accountable police service

1 Geoffrey Marshall, 'Police accountability revisited', in David Butler and A. H. Halsey (eds.), *Policy and Politics* (London: Macmillan, 1978).

2 Ronald Weitzer, *Policing under Fire: Ethnic Conflict and Police–Community Relations in Northern Ireland* (Albany: SUNY Press, 1995), p. 183.

3 Michael Brogden argues that the Police Authority, despite recent changes, is a 'publicity body for

the RUC. Its message is one-way – explaining the RUC to the community, not holding the police to account on behalf of the community.' Michael Brogden, *Two-tiered Policing: A Middle Way for Northern Ireland?* (Belfast: Democratic Dialogue, 1998), pp. 8–9.

4   Weitzer, *Policing under Fire*, p. 182; A. Hamilton, L. Moore and T. Trimble, *Policing a Divided Society: Issues and Perceptions in Northern Ireland* (Coleraine: Centre for the Study of Conflict, 1995), pp. 22–5.

5   For a discussion of the Police Authority's failure to control the use of plastic bullets, despite possessing 'authority to intervene', see Mary O'Rawe and Linda Moore, *Human Rights on Duty: Principles for Better Policing – International Lessons for Northern Ireland* (Belfast: CAJ, 1997), pp. 143–4.

6   Police Authority for Northern Ireland, *Listening to the Community, Working with the RUC* (Belfast: PANI, 1998), p. 27. Unfortunately, the Police Authority does not break down this minority (41 per cent) into Catholic and Protestant and other respondents.

7   'NI Police Authority passes vote of no confidence in chairman', *Irish Times*, Dublin, 22 February 1996.

8   Chris Ryder, *The RUC: A Force under Fire* (London: Mandarin, 1997), p. xiv.

9   Weitzer, *Policing under Fire*, p. 67 and p. 310, note 25.

10 See CAJ, *Policing the Police: A Report on the Policing of Events during the Summer of 1997 in Northern Ireland* (Belfast: CAJ, 1997); *A Submission from the Committee for the Administration of Justice (CAJ) on the Police (NI) Bill* (Belfast: CAJ, February 1998).

11 Weitzer, *Policing under Fire*, p. 185.

12 Hamilton *et al.*, *Policing a Divided Society*, p. 24. Annesley also

described the members of the Police Authority as 'a bunch of well-intentioned amateurs'. *Irish Times*, Dublin, 11 June 1998.

13 'The Authority is not aware of the exact nature of the training given to RUC Recruiting Branch staff.' PANI's memorandum to the Northern Ireland Affairs Committee, *Composition, Recruitment and Training of the RUC*, Vol. II, *Minutes of Evidence and Appendices* (London: Stationery Office, 1998), p. 45.

14 See note 5.

15 'RUC watchdog split by reform dispute', *Daily Telegraph*, London, 23 February 1996.

16 Weitzer claims that when the Police Authority was established, and despite the stipulation that it be representative, most of its senior staff came from the Stormont Ministry of Home Affairs and 'hardly reflected minority interests'. Weitzer, *Policing under Fire*, p. 65.

17 In June 1997, in the weeks before a general election, Sir Patrick Mayhew, who had been responsible for firing Ryder and Cook, appointed the Police Authority to a three-year term.

18 The only major political party with representation on the Police Authority is the UUP, with four members. PANI, *Listening to the Community*, p. 74. The other three major parties, the SDLP, Sinn Féin and the DUP, are not represented.

19 Northern Ireland Affairs Committee, *Composition, Recruitment and Training of the RUC*, p. 47.

20 Weitzer, *Policing under Fire*, p. 182.

21 Northern Ireland Affairs Committee, *Composition, Recruitment and Training of the RUC*, p. 65.

22 'Group seeks Dublin support on parades', *Irish News*, Belfast, 2 March 1998.

23 *Your Voice, Your Choice:*

Community and Police Partnership
(Belfast: Stationery Office, 1998),
p. 17.

24 As the government describes it,
'How such groups come into
existence, how they are made up
and the way in which they operate
vary, depending on the individual
circumstances of each.' *Your Voice,
Your Choice*, p. 17.

25 PANI, *Listening to the Community*,
p. 33.

26 Weitzer, *Policing under Fire*,
pp. 229–43.

27 Police Authority for Northern
Ireland, *Reflecting All Shades of
Opinion* (Belfast: PANI, 1998),
p. 15.

28 The CAJ described the draft
legislation as a 'modest proposal
which, if anything, increases
police powers rather than renders
them properly subject to civic and
political oversight'. CAJ,
Submission . . . on the Police (NI) Bill,
p. 2.

29 For details see note 23 above.

30 The unelected Police Authority
objects to the idea of an elected
authority on the grounds that this
'could produce a highly
politicised body opening the door
to partisan political control of
policing, something the
Authority was created to avoid'.
PANI, *Listening to the Community*,
p. 54.

31 The government did not use the
opportunity provided by the
Police (Northern Ireland) Act
1998 to change the Police
Authority's decision-making
rules. The act specifies that 'every
question at a meeting of the Police
Authority shall be determined by
a majority of the votes of the
members present and voting on
the question'. Schedule 1, Section
5 (2). This negligence suggests
that the spirit of the Good Friday
Agreement, with its cross-
community procedures for the
Assembly, has not flowed into

public administration.

32 In *Your Voice, Your Choice* the
government cites expense as a
possible reason for avoiding
elections to a police authority.
The document warns that the cost
of the elections to the Northern
Ireland Forum was £1.5 million,
and implicitly suggests that the
cost of electing a police authority
would be similar, p. 11. There is
no reason why such elections need
be held separately from other
elections.

33 This is recommended by Trevor
Jones and Tim Newburn,
'Policing and disaffected
communities', in Standing
Advisory Commission on
Human Rights, *Report for 1995–
1996* (London: HMSO, 1996),
p. 268.

34 Under South Africa's new Police
Act, the police are required to
consult with local communities
and to demonstrate local customer
satisfaction with the policing
service. Michael Brogden, 'An
agenda for post-Troubles policing
in Northern Ireland: the South
African precedent', in *Policing in a
New Society* (Belfast: Centre for
Research and Documentation,
1994), p. 24.

35 McGuinness was referring to the
dangers of an elected police
authority. See 'Nationalists say
paper on policing inadequate',
Irish Times, Dublin, 10 February
1998.

36 PANI, *Listening to the Community*,
p. 54.

37 The Good Friday Agreement
states that 'key decisions' are to be
taken by cross-community
procedures, either by 'parallel
consent' (where a measure is
supported by a majority of
members voting, including a
majority of the designated
unionists and nationalists) or by
'weighted majority' (where 60 per
cent of members support a

measure, including at least 40 per cent of each of the designated nationalists and unionists who vote). The government could designate all policing matters as 'key decisions', or alternatively, and with the same effect, they could be designated under the Assembly's rules as such, if at least 30 of the Assembly's 108 members say so. For further discussion see Brendan O'Leary, 'The nature of the Agreement' (the Ninth John Whyte Memorial Lecture), forthcoming in *Scottish Affairs* and *New Left Review*.

38 Even the presentation of the Police Authority's publications does not seem designed to win the hearts or minds of nationalists. The cover of *Reflecting All Shades of Opinion* shows a solitary green crayon virtually surrounded by three orange crayons, and three other crayons of red, white and blue. *Listening to the Community* portrays Northern Ireland with each county in different bright colours, seen from above and from the west. The west of Scotland, with its counties also in different bright colours, is clearly seen just beyond Northern Ireland. The only part of the Republic of Ireland that can be seen is a very small part of counties Donegal and Monaghan, both of which are coloured in the same

drab beige! Within the report the Police Authority's chairman is shown leaning against a chair, placed on a concrete floor and against a bare brick wall. Any resemblance to the Castlereagh detention centre must be presumed to be coincidental. PANI's designers might benefit from cultural sensitivity training.

39 The potential problem of 'immobilism' or deadlock in power-sharing institutions is often solved by 'log-rolling' – politicians support decisions they disagree with if it is necessary to the success of decisions they support.

40 Colin Irwin, *The Search for a Settlement: The People's Choice* (Belfast: Fortnight Educational Trust, 1998), p. 10.

41 The inventory of our proposals is contained in Appendix B. We submitted a slightly different version to the Patten Commission in September 1998.

Appendix A

*   This appendix sets out the provisions on police reform contained in the Good Friday Agreement agreed on 10 April 1998 by the participants in the multi-party talks at Stormont.

Index